Hands- On Liferay DXP

Learn Portlet Development and Customization Using OSGi Modules

Apoorva Prakash
Shaik Inthiyaz Basha

Apress®

Hands- On Liferay DXP: Learn Portlet Development and Customization Using OSGi Modules

Apoorva Prakash
BANGALORE, India

Shaik Inthiyaz Basha
Nellore, AP, India

ISBN-13 (pbk): 978-1-4842-8562-6
https://doi.org/10.1007/978-1-4842-8563-3

ISBN-13 (electronic): 978-1-4842-8563-3

Managing Director, Apress Media LLC: Welmoed Spahr
Acquisitions Editor: Divya Modi
Development Editor: James Markham
Coordinating Editor: Divya Modi

Cover designed by eStudioCalamar

Cover image designed by Pixabay

Distributed to the book trade worldwide by Springer Science+Business Media New York, 1 New York Plaza, Suite 4600, New York, NY 10004-1562, USA. Phone 1-800-SPRINGER, fax (201) 348-4505, e-mail orders-ny@springer-sbm.com, or visit www.springeronline.com. Apress Media, LLC is a California LLC and the sole member (owner) is Springer Science + Business Media Finance Inc (SSBM Finance Inc). SSBM Finance Inc is a **Delaware** corporation.

For information on translations, please e-mail booktranslations@springernature.com; for reprint, paperback, or audio rights, please e-mail bookpermissions@springernature.com.

Apress titles may be purchased in bulk for academic, corporate, or promotional use. eBook versions and licenses are also available for most titles. For more information, reference our Print and eBook Bulk Sales web page at http://www.apress.com/bulk-sales.

Any source code or other supplementary material referenced by the author in this book is available to readers on GitHub. For more detailed information, please visit https://www.apress.com/us/services/source-code.

Printed on acid-free paper

To my father,
Dr. Om Prakash Srivastava,
to whom I owe everything,
and
who inspired me but is not here to read this.
Yes, life is like that sometimes!
— Apoorva Prakash

Table of Contents

About the Authors...ix

Acknowledgments xi

Introduction xiii

Chapter 1: OSGi Basics 1

Understanding OSGi 1

How Is OSGi Different? 2

A Deeper Look at OSGi 3

OSGi Architecture 3

OSGi Bundles 5

OSGi Bundle Rules...7

Importing and Exporting Bundles 8

OSGi Bundle Lifecycle...9

Bundle States 10

OSGi Components 12

OSGi Services...14

Service Registry 16

Declarative Services...16

Liferay's OSGi Architecture 19

OSGi Features 20

Summary..22

Chapter 2: Liferay Development Basics 23

The Liferay Workspace..23

　　Liferay Workspace Primer 24

Build Tools..26

　　Gradle 26

　　Maven...27

Introduction to Liferay Modules 29

The Blade CLI 32

Running Liferay the First Time 33

　　Running Liferay Application...34

Database Connectivity with Liferay DXP 37

Gogo Shell..42

Summary...44

Chapter 3: Portlet Module Development 45

Introduction to Portlets 45

Portlet Specifications...47

Portlet Lifecycle 47

Portlet Modes and Window States 50

　　Portlet Mode 51

　　Window States...51

Java Standard Portlets...52

　　A Closer Look at HelloApressPortlet 56

Liferay Portlet Module (MVC Portlet)..58

　　Creating a Sample Liferay MVC Portlet...59

　　Understanding the Liferay MVC Portlet Controller 64

　　Understanding the Different URLs in the Liferay MVC Portlet......................67

Understanding Different Commands in the Liferay MVC Portlet....................82

Implementing Window State..96

Introduction to Other Portlet Modules..98

The Spring MVC Portlet...98

Liferay Soy Portlet 99

JSF Portlet...99

Bean Portlet...99

Gogo Shell in Action 100

Gogo Shell from the Liferay Control Panel.......................................103

Gogo Shell from the Blade CLI..104

Summary...105

Chapter 4: Advanced Liferay Concepts................................107

Inter-Portlet Communication 107

IPC via Public Render Parameters 108

IPC via Private Session Attributes...117

IPC via Server-Side Events 123

Client-Side IPC via Ajax 131

Client-Side IPC via Cookies 132

Liferay Message Bus..133

Synchronous Message Bus 140

Asynchronous Message Bus..142

Liferay Scheduler...145

Summary...149

Chapter 5: Service Builder Concepts.................................151

Introduction to the Service Builder 151

Generating Services...153

Deep Diving Into the Code Generated by the Service Builder 164

Customization via Implementation Classes 165

Remote Service Implementation 171

CRUD Operations 173

Finders 176

Dynamic Query 179

Custom SQL 181

Working with Remote Services 185

    Headless REST APIs 185

    Plain Web/REST Services 191

Summary 194

Chapter 6: Liferay Customization 195

Overriding Language Keys 195

    Global Language Property 196

    Module Language Property 198

Customizing JSPs 200

    Customization JSPs with Liferay APIs 201

    Using OSGi Fragments or a Custom JSP Bag 207

Customizing Services Using Wrappers 212

Customizing OSGi Services 218

Customizing MVC Commands 220

Customizing Models Using Model Listeners 226

Expando Attributes 229

Pre and Post-Actions 236

Customizing Search 240

Summary 245

Index 247

About the Authors

Apoorva Prakash is a Liferay-certified professional who has worked on Liferay for over a decade. Currently, he works with Schneider Electric Pvt Ltd., India, as a Liferay Expert and Engineering Lead for a team working on various projects of different technologies, including NodeJS, Python, AWS-based serverless technologies, and so on. Apoorva has defined the architecture of multiple portals, including large employee portals, ecommerce sites, and so on, in Liferay for over 12 years and counting. His other work areas include NodeJS, Python, AWS, and Kubernetes. Development and deployment are his passions, and he is inherently very keen on attention to detail. He is an avid blogger, and his blog has been mentioned in the Liferay community round-up several times. Apoorva has completed his master's degree in computer application from the school of computer science, Apeejay Institute of Technology, Greater Noida, Uttar Pradesh. His other hobbies are tech blogging and wildlife photography.

ABOUT THE AUTHORS

Shaik Inthiyaz Basha is a Liferay Architect and Technical Expert at Schneider Electric Pvt Ltd., India. He is an expert in Content Management Systems (CMS) and Amazon Web Service (AWS). Inthiyaz currently holds the position of Platform Architect in a group involved in developing Liferay and Elastic Search applications. His accomplishments in enhancing and creating various Liferay components are evident from his various successful implementations. His experience and knowledge are supported by certificates such as Liferay Backend Developer (DXP). Inthiyaz is also the founder of the `https://letuslearnliferay.blogspot.com`, which contains a lot of information on Liferay and the CMS world. Since 2011, he has created various kinds of CMS applications, supporting large banking and financial systems. His main area of interest is web applications. Inthiyaz uses Java, AWS, and Elastic Search on a daily basis, but he is open to learning other technologies and solutions. He holds a master's degree in Computer Networks from Quba College of Eng & Tech, Affiliated with JNTUA University, Nellore, Andhra Pradesh, India.

Acknowledgments

In life, one rarely comes across people whose few words or mere presence can bolster you to do something extraordinary. Many people encouraged us and contributed in innumerable ways when writing this book. We want to acknowledge the following key people whose humble support was a constant source of strength during the toil of creating this book:

- Mr. Sanju Varghese Raju

- Senior General Manager, Schneider Electric Pvt Ltd.

- One of the most humble and most genuine person we've met and we thank him for his continuous support, from inception to publishing this book.

- Mr. Veera Vasantha Reddy

- Assistant Vice President, Development Bank of Singapore.

  A technocrat and dear friend, and we thank him for his guidance and critical review comments.

- Our families

- For allowing us to burn the midnight oil and spend weekends on this book.

Introduction

Liferay has been a market leader in ready-to-deploy portals for quite some time. During its lifetime, Liferay has experienced several architectural upgrades that enhanced user and development experiences. Liferay DXP is the most mature version of Liferay. As Liferay matured, it kept adding several technologies; the biggest of which are OSGi and Gradle. OSGi added a layer of modularity to Liferay, whereas Gradle has given the deployment process more flexibility.

This book is a perfect fit for you if you possess basic Java knowledge and are familiar with the Liferay user interface. It's perfect if you want to develop portlet modules in Liferay DXP and customize the default Liferay behavior. You will also learn about OSGi, Blade CLI, the Liferay development environment setup, and best practices. This book will help improve your productivity. If you are hands-on with an older version of Liferay or have little understanding of Liferay's development approach and are looking forward to learning about the nitty-gritty of Liferay—DXP development—this book is a perfect fit for you.

Portlets are the heart and soul of Liferay development, and they can be created using multiple templates such as LiferayMVC, Spring, and others. Portlets are the endpoint for users, from where they can trigger different functionalities, such as database connectivity, IPC, schedulers, and so on.

Liferay is not all about custom development; you can also use its out-of-the-box functionalities to achieve requirements. To utilize its out-of-the-box functionality, you can customize Liferay default behavior in several ways, including customization of user interfaces, languages, action classes, events, services, and other aspects. Liferay's out-of-the-box search framework can also be used to enable search in custom entities.

We tried to cover all concepts related to hands-on Liferay development and sincerely hope the book fulfills our readers' expectations.

Source Code

All source code used in this book can be downloaded from github. com/Apress/Hands--On-Liferay-DXP-by-Apoorva-Prakash-and-Inthiyaz-Basha.

CHAPTER 1

OSGi Basics

This chapter dives deep into OSGi concepts, along with its essential features, its architecture, services, the Service Registry, and a few other crucial topics that fall under the basics of OSGi concerning Liferay DXP. Further, you learn about bundles with a straightforward example in the next chapters. By the end of this chapter, you will understand the unlimited potential of OSGi.

Understanding OSGi

The Open Services Gateway Initiative (OSGi) was founded in March, 1999 and is managed by the OSGi Alliance.

The OSGi Alliance now refers to the framework specification as OSGi or the OSGi Service Platform. To create a Java-based service framework that can be managed remotely, the vendors of networking providers and embedded systems came together and created a set of standards. OSGi was initially developed to be a gateway for managing Internet-enabled devices like smart appliances. The Java software framework is embedded in a gateway hardware platform, such as a set-top box or cable modem. This software framework acts as a central message dealer to the home's LAN (Local Area Network). The core goal is to efficiently manage cross-dependencies for software developers by creating a standardized middleware for intelligent devices.

© Apoorva Prakash and Shaik Inthiyaz Basha 2022
A. Prakash and S. I. Basha, *Hands- On Liferay DXP*,
https://doi.org/10.1007/978-1-4842-8563-3_1

Liferay uses OSGi extensively for product development. Other noteworthy companies include Oracle WebLogic, Eclipse Foundation, IBM WebSphere, Atlassian Jira and Confluence, and JBoss. These are the notable companies that are using OSGi for their product development.

Let's look at what makes OSGi different from other frameworks.

How Is OSGi Different?

The OSGi framework is different from other frameworks based on Java, especially Spring. More than one application can exist in the same container in the OSGi bundle runtime environment. The OSGi container takes care of access to the dependencies required by each component in the container. The OSGi framework also supports standardized dependency injection, as defined by the Aries Blueprint project.

In OSGi, bundles can consume services exposed to other bundles. A bundle can define and declare a version of bundles. The runtime will automatically load all its bundles to resolve all dependencies.

Note   In OSGi, if any bundle dependencies require multiple versions of the same bundle, they are also available side by side.

OSGi is a modularity layer for the Java platform. OSGi's core specifications define a component and service model for Java. OSGi provides a service-oriented development model, allowing for a service-oriented architecture within a virtual machine.

For example, large Java applications can be challenging to deploy and manage. In order to update deployment, the system/servers need to be cycled, and the application build and deployment may cause system outages. But OSGi provides an isolated module cycling/updating capability to increase availability.

A Deeper Look at OSGi

OSGi offers an elegant solution for handling dependencies, by requiring dependency declarations within units of modularity. Multiple applications can coexist in the same container in OSGi, and the OSGi bundle runtime environment manages them. The OSGi container will ensure each component is sufficiently isolated and approach any dependencies required to access.

OSGi has two parts. The first part is called the *bundle*. It has modular component specifications, which are generally referred to as *plugins*. The specification will help determine the bundle's interaction and lifecycle infrastructure. The second part is the *Service Registry,* which is beneficial to understanding how bundles discover, publish, and bind to services in the Service Oriented Architecture (SOA) at the Java Virtual Machine (JVM) level.

OSGi Architecture

The OSGi architecture is used in different Java-based applications. It is illustrated in Figure 1-1 and consists of several layers that work on top of the hardware and operating system:

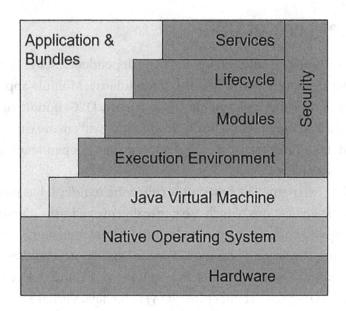

Figure 1-1. *OSGI service gateway*

- **Bundles**: An OSGi bundle is a Java ARchive (JAR) file that contains resources, Java code, and a manifest that describes the bundle and its dependencies. For an application, the OSGi bundle is the unit of deployment. You learn more about bundles in the next section of the chapter.

- **Services**: The services layer in the OSGi architecture will offer a "publish find bind" model for old Java objects to connect bundles dynamically. To simplify, an OSGi service is a Java object instance registered to an OSGi framework with a set of properties.

- **Lifecycle**: The lifecycle layer provides the API used to start, install, uninstall, update, and stop objects.

- **Modules**: This layer defines how to export and import code by bundle.

- **Security**: This layer handles the security aspects.

- **Execution Environment**: This layer defines the available classes and methods in a specific platform.

Now that you've learned a bit about the OSGi basics, the next section explores OSGi bundles.

OSGi Bundles

Bundles are modular Java components. Creating and managing bundles is facilitated by OSGi, and bundles can be deployed in a container. A developer uses OSGi specifications and tools to create one or more bundles. The bundle's lifecycle is defined and managed by OSGi. It also supports the bundles' interactions and hosts them in a container. The OSGi container is roughly parallel to a JVM. Similarly, bundles can be treated as Java applications with distinctive abilities. OSGi bundles run as client and server components inside the OSGi container.

So, bundles are nothing more than OSGi components, and they are in the form of standard JAR files. The only difference between regular JAR files and bundles is the *manifest header* (also referred to as *bundle identifiers*). These manifest headers tell the runtime that this JAR is not a standard JAR file but an OSGi bundle. These bundle identifiers consist of two main parts—Bundle-SymbolicName and Bundle-Version. You must use a combination of these two to export and import the services. This combination of Bundle-SymbolicName and Bundle-Version (semantic versioning) creates a unique identifier for OSGi bundles and thus for dependencies.

Note   Logically, a bundle has an independent lifecycle with a piece of functionality. It can work independently with start, stop, and remove.

Technically, a bundle is a JAR file containing some OSGi-specific headers in the `MANIFEST.MF` file.

As depicted here, the `Bundle-SymbolicName` is `com.handsonliferay.employee.portlet` and the `Bundle-Version` is `1.2.3.2022`.

Bundle-Name: handsonliferay-employee-portlet
Bundle-SymbolicName: com.handsonliferay.employee.portlet
Bundle-Version: 1.2.3.2022
Export-Package: com.handsonliferay.employee

Let's deep dive into understanding them:

- `Bundle-SymbolicName`: A unique identifier that refers to the bundle. This is generally understandable human text so that developers can understand the functionality written inside it. The best practice is to name it as class packages are named. In the previous example, you created an API with the symbolic name `com.handsonliferay.employee.portlet`, which any OSGi bundle can import to consume the exposed services. This naming convention is a standard Liferay development approach.

- `Bundle-Version`: 1.2.3.2022. There are four parts to a version number, each separated by three dots (see Figure 1-2). This versioning scheme is also known as *bundle semantic versioning*. Let's look at part of the semantic versioning process:

- *Major*, which is 1 in this case. The major version is changed when there are code changes that can break the code used in the APIs of this bundle.

- *Minor*, which is 2 in this example. This means there are API changes in the bundle, which may include some fixes. It refers to APIs of this bundle and it will not break the code.

- *Micro*, which is 3 is this example. This changes when there are minor changes and no compatibility issues.

- *Qualifier*, which is used when there is no impact to compatibility. It's used to tag snapshots or nightly builds.

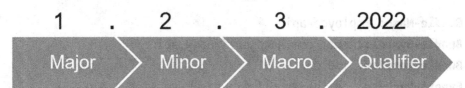

Figure 1-2. *Bundle version*

OSGi Bundle Rules

With these details, you can now learn how OSGI bundles are supposed to work in real-time. Let's look at the OSGI bundle rules:

1. You want code that may include or exclude some application configuration. Using this approach, you will get the primary benefit of modularity.

2. You want code that should update independently from other code. Using this approach, you get another primary benefit of modularity.

3. You want code that has a set of specific dependencies on other libraries. This way, you decrease the chance of conflicts by isolating those dependencies.

4. Some of the interface code might have different implementations. This way, without making any other changes, you can swap out implementations.

Importing and Exporting Bundles

The following example exports a service called `com.handsonliferay.employee.api` with version 1.0.0. The Employee API is exposed with a `Symbolic-Name` of `com.handsonliferay.employee.api` and a version number of `1.0.0`:

```
Bundle-Name: Employee-api
Bundle-SymbolicName: com.handsonliferay.api
Bundle-Version: 1.0.0
Export-Package: com.handsonliferay.api; version=1.0.0
```

Importing Bundles

To understand bundle importing, you must understand version ranges. As you have already learned, an OSGi bundle can be exported with a specific version number, so multiple OSGi bundles have the same symbolic name but different versions. They are essentially nothing but different versions of the same OSGi bundle. There may be cases when you have more than one valid bundle version from various deployed OSGi bundles. To solve this scenario, you can mention ranges in the `import` statement. Square brackets and parentheses are used for this purpose. Square brackets denote inclusiveness, whereas parentheses indicate exclusiveness. You can see this with the following example:

[2.1, 3.0) means include version 2.1 up to, but not including, 3.0.

Import-Package: com.handsonliferay.employee; version="[2.1,3.0)"

This section has explained the basics of OSGi bundles; in the next section, you explore the OSGi bundle lifecycle.

OSGi Bundle Lifecycle

OSGi is a very dynamic platform, and bundles are the core of this mechanism. A bundle is a state-aware unit, meaning a bundle has several states that it can traverse through and know what state it is in. In traditional OSGi, you have a BundleActivator, where you have start() and stop() methods that are invoked upon the start and stop of the bundle, respectively.

Note   Activators are nothing but classes that implement the org. osgi.framework.BundleActivator interface.

The OSGi bundle lifecycle layer puts on bundles that can be dynamically started, installed, updated, stopped, and uninstalled. These bundles depend on the module layer for class loading, but it will add an API to manage modules at runtime. See Listing 1-1.

Listing 1-1. Bundle Activator Class

```
package com.handsonliferay.employee.osgi;

import org.osgi.framework.BundleActivator;
import org.osgi.framework.BundleContext;
```

```java
public class Activator implements BundleActivator{

        @Override
        public void start(BundleContext context) throws
        Exception {
                System.out.println("Starting Hands On
                Liferay");
        }

        @Override
        public void stop(BundleContext context) throws
        Exception {
        System.out.println("Stopping Hands on Liferay");

        }

}
```

Bundle States

Now that you understand that the bundle is state-aware and uses the start and stop methods of a BundleActivator, it's time to look at all the possible states that the OSGi bundle can traverse through (see Figure 1-3).

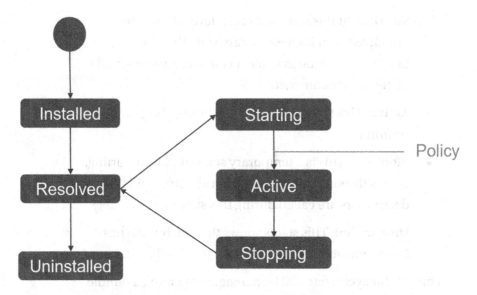

Figure 1-3. *Bundle states*

- **Installed**: This state depicts that the bundle has
  entered the OSGi runtime. Nothing else; it's not
  available; running or resolving the dependencies
  means a bundle is available in the OSGi runtime. If a
  bundle stays in this state for a long time, that means
  that it's waiting for some of the bundle's dependencies
  to be met.

- **Resolved**: This state shows that the bundle has been
  installed successfully, and the OSGi runtime resolves
  all the dependencies with the help of the installed
  bundles in the OSGi runtime. The bundle is available
  for the next stage, which is Start. Sometimes, the
  runtime will skip this state if a bundle is started by
  getting all the required dependencies.

- **Starting**: At this state, the entry-level classes are initialized, and it's a temporary state that the bundle goes through while it is starting and once all dependencies are met.

- **Active**: This state shows that the bundle is up and running.

- **Stopping**: This is a temporary state similar to starting; it goes through this when the bundle stops. All the destructors are called during this state.

- **Uninstalled**: This states shows that the bundle has been removed successfully from the OSGi container.

A bundle lifecycle state will be managed, meaning a bundle can change its state by itself upon deployment, and developers and administrators can manage its state. There are various GUI and command-line tools available to do this. Gogo shell and Apache Felix are two of the most popular tools. You'll see these tools in detail in later chapters.

This section has explained the OSGi bundle lifecycle; in the next section, you explore the OSGi components.

OSGi Components

Any Java class inside a bundle can be declared a component. This can be achieved with the help of declarative services (DS), which provide a service component model on top of the OSGi services. A component can publish itself as a service and make itself available to other components. Similarly, it can consume services published by already installed components.

OSGi components have an independent lifecycle and are reusable, which means you can stop them and start them again without reinstalling them. They will traverse through their lifecycle events again and again. They can have properties and activation policies. An OSGi bundle can have lifecycle methods for activation, deactivation, and configuration.

DS service components are marked with the @Component annotation; they implement or extend a service class. These service components can refer to and use each other's services. The Service Component Runtime (SCR) registers component services and handles them by binding them to other components that reference them.

There are two parts to this process—service registration and service handling.

- **Service registration**: When a module containing a service component is installed, the SCR creates a config, binds it with the specified service type, and makes a reference in the Service Registry.

- **Service handling**: When a module referencing a service exposed from another module is installed, SCR searches the Service Registry for a component whose configuration matches the required service type. Once the component is found, SCR binds an instance of that service to the referring member.

Note   To understand in a nutshell, you can say—when a module with an exposed service is deployed, SCR registers it in the Service Registry and when a module importing a service is deployed, SCR searches for it in the Service Registry and returns its instance.

@Component annotation is a declaration to make the class an OSGi component. @Referance annotation marks a field to be injected with a service, and once the Service Registry finds the essential service, it is injected with the resolved service. It can only be used in a @Component class.

Note   For example, a class with a declarative services component, @Component, can use @Reference to bind to another OSGi service.

Let's look at an OSGi component with an example; refer to Listing 1-2.

Listing 1-2. OSGi @Component Declaration

```
package com.apress.handsonliferay.portlet;

import com.handsonliferay.apress_service_builder.model.
ApressBook;
@Component(
        immediate = true,
        service = EmpolyeeService.class
)
public class Employee implements EmpolyeeService {
}
```

This section has explained the OSGi component; in the next section, you explore OSGi services.

OSGi Services

An OSGi service is a Java class or interface and a service property, shown as name or value pairs. The OSGi service is nothing but a component registered to an OSGi container Service Registry (SR) by the Service Component Runtime (SCR). Listings 1-3 and 1-4 show how the service interface is declared and implemented.

Listing 1-3. Service Interface

```
package com.handsonliferay.service.api;
public interface EmployeeService{
        public String getEmpName();
        public void setEmpName(String name);
}
```

Listing 1-4. Service Implementation

```
package com.handsonliferay.service.Impl;

import com.handsonliferay.employee.api.EmployeeService;
import org.osgi.service.component.annotations.Component;

@Component(
                immediate = true,
                service = EmpolyeeService.class
        )

public class EmployeeServiceImpl implements EmployeeService{
        @Override
        public String getEmpName() {
                return _name;
        }

        @Override
        public void setEmpName(String name) {
                _name = name;
        }
}
```

Service Registry

The service layer contains a Service Registry and within that framework, services will be registered and used by other applications and clients. In the Service Registry, a bundle can register an implementation of a service. Lookup is performed via a Java interface and service properties by the bundles.

A bundle is responsible for the runtime service dependency management activities, including discovery, publication, and binding, as well as adapting to changes resulting from the dynamic of services in the bundle. Service providers and service requestors are both part of a bundle in OSGi.

- In the Service Registry, service providers publish their services.

- To find the services and bind to service providers, service requestors use the Service Registry.

It provides a mechanism to publish services to an OSGi container and dynamically look up and bind published services. It will hide the client's implementation details, which will give loose coupling, and consuming clients may have the policies and filters for binding specific implementations.

Declarative Services

Declarative services are how OSGi handles problems due to instantiation. If you want to create two interfaces, instantiate classes using them, and provide a concrete instance of an interface, you need some way. Declarative services are the way to do this with less code implementation. An OSGi declarative service is also called a Service Component Runtime (SCR).

OSGi will also support XML configuration; this configuration is similar to the configuration that the Spring Framework supports. When you drop an XML configuration file into the OSGI-INF/ path inside your bundle JAR file, the parsing will happen automatically once the OSGi container starts the bundle. It allows you to declare and consume services via XML metadata and annotations. Figures 1-4 and 1-5 show how a bundle is registered in the Service Registry.

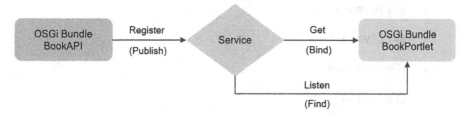

Figure 1-4. *Service Registry process*

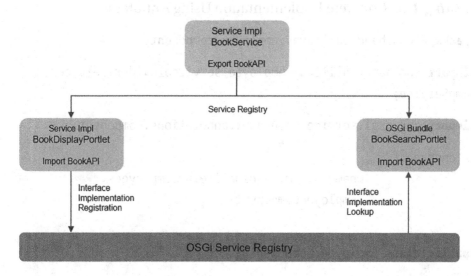

Figure 1-5. *OSGi Service Registry*

17

You must use the following header in the bundle's MANIFEST file to identify the XML file by OSGi service component runtime:

Service-Component: OSGI-INF/com. handsonliferay.employees.configuration.xml

The standard declarative service annotations are listed here:

- @Component

- @Reference

- @Activate

- @Deactivate

- @Modified

A concrete example is shown in Listing 1-5.

Listing 1-5. Concrete Implementation Using Annotation

```
package com.handsonliferay.employee.component;

import com.handsonliferay.employee.serviceprovider.services.
EmpService;

import org.osgi.service.component.annotations.Component;

@Component(
            name = com.handsonliferay.employees.
            EmployeeComponent
    )

public class EmployeesComponent {

    @Activate
    public void activate() {
            System.out.println( "Component is Activated");
    }
```

```
@Deactivate
public void deactivate() {
        System.out.println( "Component is
        Deactivated");
}

@Modified
public void modified() {
        System.out.println( "Component is Modified" );
}

@Reference
public void setEmpService(Empservice empservice) {
        System.out.println( "Component is
        setService()" );
        System.out.println( empservice.greetHello());
}
}
```

This section has explained the OSGi services; in the next section, you learn about Liferay's OSGi architecture.

Liferay's OSGi Architecture

You should now understand what an OSGi container is and how bundles and services work inside it. It's time to look at how Liferay DXP is designed to have an embedded OSGi container to leverage OSGi features. All Liferay DXP applications, be it portlets, services, hooks, or anything else, are OSGi applications (bundle components), so they run inside embedded OSGi containers. But this does not mean standard OSGi applications cannot run inside; they can work well inside Liferay DXP's OSGi container as well.

In the straightforward standard OSGi environment, an OSGi container works inside the Java runtime, and all the OSGi bundles run inside the OSGi container. But in the case of Liferay DXP, which embeds an OSGi container, there are two more layers between the Servlet container (Tomcat or any other server) and the Liferay Web application. Most of the services and functionalities in Liferay DXP leverage the OSGi component and service model. Figure 1-6 helps to elucidate this model.

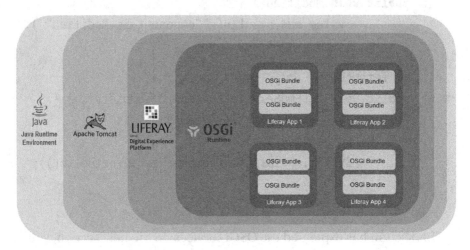

Figure 1-6. *Liferay OSGi architecture*

This section has explained Liferay's OSGi architecture; in the next section, you explore the main OSGi features.

OSGi Features

The OSGi application framework defines a standard dependency injection mechanism for Java components. This dependency injection mechanism is driven from the Spring Framework and is extended declaratively to register components in OSGi interfaces as services in OSGi SR. This is one of the most valuable features of OSGi.

OSGi uses a different kind of model for assembling bundles. OSGi tools include a model for assembling an application into a deployable unit. The unit may consist of several bundles and must consist of metadata that describes the version and dependencies.

The OSGi tools also include extensions beyond the OSGi Enterprise Expert Group specifications to provide complete integration of OSGi modularity with Java enterprise technologies.

To overcome the issues faced by applications of Java EE, OSGi modularity provides standard mechanisms. Here are the benefits provided by the OSGi framework:

- OSGI provides adaptable changing requirements; applications are portable and easier to reengineer.

- The framework provides a standardized form as part of the application server runtime, rather than a third-party library to the declarative assembly and simplified unit test of the Spring Framework.

- The framework allows you to deploy a web application as a set of versioned OSGi bundles with a dynamic lifecycle to integrate with the Java EE programming model.

- Application bundle dependencies and versions administration are also supported.

- OSGI also supports simplifying and standardizing third-party library integration.

- OSGI applications have the capability of accessing external bundle repositories.

21

- The framework also provides isolation for enterprise applications composed of different versioned bundles with dynamic lifecycles.

- The framework strengthens service-oriented design at the module level.

Summary

In this chapter, you explored the essential features of OSGi, including its architecture, its services and Service Registry, and a few other crucial topics that fall under the basics of OSGi with respect to Liferay DXP. You also explored bundles with a straightforward example, which should be enough to grasp the potential of OSGi. However, OSGi is a vast specification, so we encourage you to explore more on the Internet.

CHAPTER 2

Liferay Development Basics

This chapter focuses on explaining the Liferay development basics. You learn about the Liferay workspace's power to set up your local development environments and its fundamentals for creating, building, and deploying Liferay modules using different approaches, such as the wizard and the Blade CLI. The chapter also explains how to build modules using Gradle and Maven. Once you are familiar with these fundamentals, you learn how to start the Liferay DXP Server and connect your Liferay DXP instance to the database. Lastly, you are introduced to Gogo shell for managing deployed modules.

The Liferay Workspace

As the name suggests, a Liferay workplace is nothing more than an area to keep and manage projects while developing modules in Liferay DXP. The Liferay workplace is generated to help manage Liferay modules by providing the right set of tools and folder structure and offering support to build processes and other configurations. In the Liferay documentation, the workspace is called a "generated wrapper environment" and is an official way to create Liferay DXP modules using Gradle. However, the Liferay workplace can also be created with Maven. Don't worry if you don't know Gradle and Maven; you'll learn more about them later in this chapter.

© Apoorva Prakash and Shaik Inthiyaz Basha 2022
A. Prakash and S. I. Basha, *Hands- On Liferay DXP*,
https://doi.org/10.1007/978-1-4842-8563-3_2

Liferay Workspace Primer

The Liferay workspace is very flexible, as it can be used in many different development environments. Typically, when a team is working on a Liferay project, the Liferay workspace is initialized by one developer and then committed to a revision control system. Then the same workspace is checked out by the rest of the team and configured in the Eclipse/Liferay Developer Studio to develop new modules. However, one project can have multiple workspaces depending on its requirements. Also, it can be used in various IDEs. Build scripts and configurations can also be edited and easily managed using the Liferay workspace. Not only this, but the workspace can be customized according to need. So, a team of developers can share a single Liferay workspace, which is why it's considered flexible.

Two approaches can initialize the Liferay workspace: using the Blade CLI or using the Eclipse/Liferay Developer Studio, supporting Gradle and Maven for project builds. They are covered briefly in the upcoming section.

A Liferay workspace consists of the following directory structure:

- Configs: This folder contains configuration files of different environments. These files are used by Liferay DXP servers and projects inside your workspace as global configuration files.

- Gradle: This folder contains the Gradle wrapper used by the Liferay DXP workspace.

- Modules: This folder contains Liferay DXP custom modules.

- Themes: This folder contains the Liferay themes generated using the Liferay Theme Generator.

- Build.gradle: This folder is a standard build file of Gradle.

- **Gradle-local.properties**: This folder is used to specify the user-specific properties of your workspace, which will help multiple users use a single workspace by configuring specific properties for the workspace on their machines.

- **Gradle.properties**: This file specifies the Liferay DXP server global configuration and workspace's project location.

- **Gradlew**: This folder is used to execute the Gradle command wrapper.

- **Settings.gradle**: This folder configures dependencies and applies plugins to the workspace.

Figure 2-1 shows the Liferay workspace.

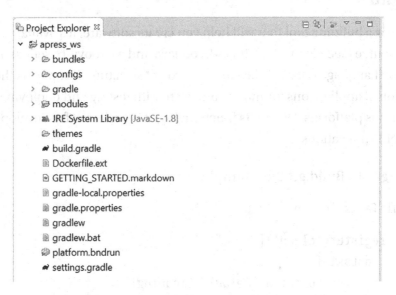

Figure 2-1. *The Liferay workspace*

You see Gradle-related folders and files here, but this does not mean that only Gradle can be used to build the modules.

This section has explained the Liferay workspace; in the next section, you explore various Liferay DXP-supported build tools.

Build Tools

Liferay DXP modules can be built using Gradle or Maven. However, by default, Gradle is used for builds. Gradle and Maven are different tools that will help you build software. Building software is an end-to-end process involving many distinct functions. Compiling the source code and packaging are the two most important in this context.

Gradle

Gradle is a building tool that will help you create software; it's available as open source (see Listing 2-1). It works on Java and a Groovy-based Domain Specific Language (DSL) to develop the project structure. It supports the creation of applications for mobile and web, with testing and deployment on various platforms. Due to its functionality, it is preferred for developing Android applications.

Listing 2-1. Build.gradle Example

```
defaultTasks 'clean', 'run'

tasks.register('clean'){
        doLast {
                println 'Default Cleaning!'
                }
}
```

```
tasks.register('run'){
        doLast {
                println 'Default Running!'
                }
}

tasks.register('run'){
        doLast {
                println 'Hands On Liferay!'
                }
}
```

Listing 2-2 shows this example's output.

Listing 2-2. The Output of the Listing 2-1

```
> gradle -q
Default Cleaning!
Default Running!
```

Maven

Maven also helps create different software in the lifecycle of Maven, and it is an open-source project management tool. It will help focus on the standardization required for software development in a standard layout within a short time. Maven uses Extensible Markup Language (XML) to structure the application (see Listing 2-3).

Listing 2-3. Pom.xml Example

```
<project xmlns="http://maven.apache.org/POM/4.0.0"
xmlns:xsi="http://www.w3.org/2001/XMLSchema-instance"
  xsi:schemaLocation="http://maven.apache.org/POM/4.0.0
http://maven.apache.org/xsd/maven-4.0.0.xsd">
```

27

```xml
<modelVersion>4.0.0</modelVersion>

<groupId>com.apress.handsonliferay</groupId>

<artifactId>handsonliferay</artifactId>
<version>0.0.1-SNAPSHOT</version>

<packaging>jar</packaging>

<name>Maven Quick Start Archetype</name>
<url>http://maven.apache.org</url>
<plugins>
        <plugin>
                <artifactId>handsonliferay</artifactId>
                <configuration>
                        <archive>
                                <manifest><mainClass>
                                hands.on.Liferay
                                </mainClass></manifest>
                        </archive>
                        <descriptionRefs>
                                <descriptionRef>
                                        jar-with-
                                        dependencies
                                </descriptionRef>
                        </descriptionRefs>
                </configuration>
                <executions>
                        <execution>
                                <id>make-
                                liferaycall</id>
                                <phase>package</phase>
```

```
                    <goals><goal>single
                    </goal></goals>
                </execution>
            </executions>
        </plugin>
    </plugins>
    <dependencies>
        <dependency>
            <groupId>junit</groupId>
            <artifactId>junit</artifactId>
            <version>4.8.2</version>
            <scope>test</scope>
        </dependency>
    </dependencies>
</project>
```

Introduction to Liferay Modules

This book has already discussed what a Liferay module actually is, but to brush up, a Liferay module is simply an OSGi component with a specific declaration for registering it as a Liferay component in the @component annotation body. The crucial entries in this annotation are the property key and the service key. There are different values for them, which you learn in detail in the Liferay portlet creation section of the next chapter. Here, you see an overview of a Liferay module.

If you break down the process of creating modules, you get the following steps:

1. **Creating an empty module**: A module consists of a folder structure that's ideal for maintaining scalable code.

2. **Creating the configuration files**: You have already created a folder structure, but to register the folder structure as a module, you need to create a few configuration files, including a manifest, build scripts, and resources.

3. **Creating the source code**: A module needs source code to implement the logic. This is the backbone of the module. It indicates when the module is deployed, when it's visible, and when it's executed to the end user.

4. **Compilation**: By the end of Step 3, you have created a module, but it is passive, which means the module is created, but it is not running. To run the module, you must build the code. Compilation is the first step of the build process. The code is built from the configuration and build scripts you created. The compiled code is packaged in a WAR or JAR file (an artifact), ready for deployment during the next step.

5. **Deployment**: Deployment is the process of installing the packaged artifact on the application server. Liferay has a straightforward installation process; you have to copy the artifact in the `deploy` directory of the application server, and the rest is taken care of by the Liferay runtime.

Blade tools and Developer Studio can be used to do all this effectively and efficiently. You learn about the Blade CLI commands needed to do these steps in the next section of this chapter.

Listing 2-4 shows the Liferay module's @component annotation as an example.

Listing 2-4. The @component Annotation

```
@Component(
        immediate = true,
        property = {
                "com.liferay.portlet.display-category=category.
                sample",
                "com.liferay.portlet.header-portlet-css=/css/
                main.css",
                "com.liferay.portlet.instanceable=true",
                "javax.portlet.display-name=ApressMVC",
                "javax.portlet.init-param.template-path=/",
                "javax.portlet.init-param.view-template=/
                view.jsp",
                "javax.portlet.name=" + ApressMVCPortletKeys.
                APRESSMVC,
                "javax.portlet.resource-bundle=content.Language",
                "javax.portlet.security-role-ref=power-user,user"
        },
        service = Portlet.class
)
```

This section has explained the various Liferay DXP-supported build tools; in the next section, you explore the Blade CLI.

The Blade CLI

Blade stands for Bootstrap Liferay Advanced Developer Environment, which essentially provides a command-line interface for managing Liferay modules and projects in a Liferay workspace. Internally, the Blade CLI is a bootstrapped version of a Gradle-based environment that creates/builds Liferay modules. Everything from creation to the deployment of modules can be done with the help of Blade commands.

Once you practice, using Blade commands is the easiest way to work with Liferay modules. Projects created via the Blade CLI can be used in any development editor or IDE, which is the most significant advantage of creating projects using the Blade CLI. The Blade CLI can be installed with the Liferay Project SDK installer. A few of the necessary commands are listed here:

- `init`: This command is used to initialize a new Liferay workspace. As you know, you need to create a workspace before creating a module. By default, all the Blade commands create a Gradle-based environment, which can be customized to Maven. It also automatically sets the default Liferay DXP version. For example:

  ```
  blade init -v 7.0 [WORKSPACE_NAME]
  ```

- `version`: This command displays version information about the Blade CLI.

- `samples`: This command generates a sample project.

- `create`: This command creates a new Liferay module project from the available templates.

- `install`: This command installs a bundle into Liferay's module framework.

- deploy: This command builds and deploys bundles to the Liferay module framework.

- update: This command updates the Blade CLI to the latest version.

- server: This command starts or stops the server defined by your Liferay project. For example:

  ```
  blade server start -b
  ```

- help: This command provides help about a specific command.

- sh: This command connects to Liferay, executes the Gogo command, and returns the output.

This section has explained how you can work with the Blade CLI; in the next section, you learn how to run Liferay DXP the first time.

Running Liferay the First Time

To superficially understand Liferay, you can broadly say that Liferay is a Java-based web application (a portal) running inside an application server. It may be in any form, such as a Liferay DXP bundled application server that can run in a cloud-based server or a container (Docker and so on). There is another way, which is to manually install Liferay in your choice of application server.

Liferay comes bundled with server applications, such as Apache Tomcat, Jboss, Glassfish, and so on. The Liferay DXP Tomcat bundle is an archive that can be extracted, configured, and run on any server. It is a very lean Apache Tomcat application server with Liferay DXP installed and can be easily configured. The example you see in this section is the installation of a Tomcat bundled Liferay DXP on a Windows computer.

Here are the prerequisites for installation:

- **Java installation**: A compatible Java (JDK) version is installed. Java 11 is recommended, or any equivalent TCK compatible Java, such as AWS Corretto. Check the Liferay compatibility matrix on the official website. The Java_home and path variables must be set.

- **Liferay artifacts**: The Tomcat bundle and activation key downloaded from Liferay's official website.

Running Liferay Application

To run the Liferay DXP Tomcat bundle, you need to extract the bundle to a location of your choice on your computer. This location is referred to as the *Liferay home*, and all the Liferay applications and Tomcat files are located inside it. You have to use files from this Liferay home directory to run the application. The top hierarchy of the application server (see Figure 2-2) contains the following folders:

- data: This folder stores files that are stored inside Liferay Documents and Media, search indexes, hypersonic databases, and the deployed license of a Liferay subscription. These are not present in all environments, but depend on the configurations.

- deploy: This directory is readable from the auto-deploy scanner and is used for deployment. Whenever a JAR file is ready, you have to move the JAR inside this directory to get it deployed.

- `elasticsearch-sidecar`: This is the embedded search engine of Liferay DXP 7.4. This was named `elasticsearch7` in version 7.3. It was not part of the bundle before Liferay DXP 7.2 and below.

- `license`: This folder contains the distribution license information of Liferay DXP and other third-party software.

- `logs`: This folder stores all the Liferay run logs.

- `osgi`: This folder contains all the artifacts and configurations of the deployed OSGi modules in the server. You can say this is the backbone of an OSGi system inside a Liferay DXP application server.

- `patching-tool`: This folder appears in the Enterprise edition of the Liferay DXP distribution only. This tool helps in installing officially published patches in the Liferay DXP application server.

- `tools`: This folder contains a script batch file, which helps in migrating the Liferay database from a lower version to the current version of Liferay when you're upgrading Liferay.

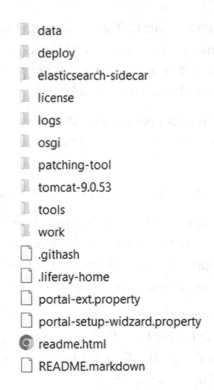

Figure 2-2. *The top hierarchy of the application server*

It helps to run the startup script bundled with your application server to run Liferay. For the Tomcat bundle, you must navigate to the bin directory in the tomcat folder and then run the startup.bat file. Doing so will open the server login command prompt, and it will take some time to start the server. Once the server starts, you'll see the screen shown in Figure 2-3.

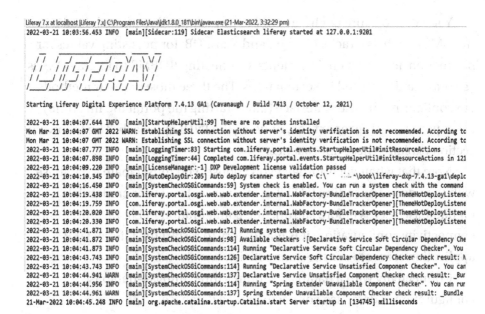

Liferay 7.x at localhost [Liferay 7.x] C:\Program Files\Java\jdk1.8.0_181\bin\javaw.exe (21-Mar-2022, 3:32:29 pm)
2022-03-21 10:03:56.453 INFO [main][Sidecar:119] Sidecar Elasticsearch liferay started at 127.0.0.1:9201

Starting Liferay Digital Experience Platform 7.4.13 GA1 (Cavanaugh / Build 7413 / October 12, 2021)

2022-03-21 10:04:07.644 INFO [main][StartupHelperUtil:99] There are no patches installed
Mon Mar 21 10:04:07 GMT 2022 WARN: Establishing SSL connection without server's identity verification is not recommended. According to
Mon Mar 21 10:04:07 GMT 2022 WARN: Establishing SSL connection without server's identity verification is not recommended. According to
2022-03-21 10:04:07.777 INFO [main][LoggingTimer:83] Starting com.liferay.portal.events.StartupHelperUtil#initResourceActions
2022-03-21 10:04:07.898 INFO [main][LoggingTimer:44] Completed com.liferay.portal.events.StartupHelperUtil#initResourceActions in 121
2022-03-21 10:04:09.220 INFO [main][LicenseManager:-1] DXP Development license validation passed
2022-03-21 10:04:10.345 INFO [main][AutoDeployDir:205] Auto deploy scanner started for C:\`  ` -\book\liferay-dxp-7.4.13-ga1\deplc
2022-03-21 10:04:16.450 INFO [main][SystemCheckOSGiCommands:59] System check is enabled. You can run a system check with the command
2022-03-21 10:04:19.438 INFO [com.liferay.portal.osgi.web.wab.extender.internal.WabFactory-BundleTrackerOpener][ThemeHotDeployListene
2022-03-21 10:04:19.759 INFO [com.liferay.portal.osgi.web.wab.extender.internal.WabFactory-BundleTrackerOpener][ThemeHotDeployListene
2022-03-21 10:04:20.020 INFO [com.liferay.portal.osgi.web.wab.extender.internal.WabFactory-BundleTrackerOpener][ThemeHotDeployListene
2022-03-21 10:04:20.330 INFO [com.liferay.portal.osgi.web.wab.extender.internal.WabFactory-BundleTrackerOpener][ThemeHotDeployListene
2022-03-21 10:04:41.871 INFO [main][SystemCheckOSGiCommands:71] Running system check
2022-03-21 10:04:41.872 INFO [main][SystemCheckOSGiCommands:98] Available checkers :[Declarative Service Soft Circular Dependency Che
2022-03-21 10:04:41.873 INFO [main][SystemCheckOSGiCommands:114] Running "Declarative Service Soft Circular Dependency Checker". You
2022-03-21 10:04:43.743 INFO [main][SystemCheckOSGiCommands:126] Declarative Service Soft Circular Dependency Checker check result: N
2022-03-21 10:04:43.743 INFO [main][SystemCheckOSGiCommands:114] Running "Declarative Service Unsatisfied Component Checker". You can
2022-03-21 10:04:44.941 WARN [main][SystemCheckOSGiCommands:137] Declarative Service Unsatisfied Component Checker check result: _Bur
2022-03-21 10:04:44.956 INFO [main][SystemCheckOSGiCommands:114] Running "Spring Extender Unavailable Component Checker". You can run
2022-03-21 10:04:44.961 WARN [main][SystemCheckOSGiCommands:137] Spring Extender Unavailable Component Checker check result: _Bundle
21-Mar-2022 10:04:45.248 INFO [main] org.apache.catalina.startup.Catalina.start Server startup in [134745] milliseconds

Figure 2-3. *The Liferay server startup*

This section has explained how to start the Liferay server the first time;
the next section explains how to connect the server to a database.

Database Connectivity with Liferay DXP

Database connectivity is essential for any web application. The Liferay
DXP database stores a lot of information, including user data, site data,
and so on. It may shock you, but in a fresh installation of Liferay DXP, you
get approximately 392 tables. In fact, starting Liferay DXP (or any version
of Liferay) is not at all possible without a database. Due to this reason,
Liferay DXP is shipped with an embedded in-memory database, which is
initialized with sample data when you start the server the first time. The
name of this in-memory database is Hypersonic SQL (HSQL). The HSQL
database is recommended for demo purposes or the first startup only, as it
loses values when Liferay is restarted.

You need to connect Liferay DXP to any standard relational database (RDBMS), such as Oracle, MySQL, and MariaDB, for persisting values for production and other environments. Connecting RDBMS to Liferay DXP is very easy and achieved in several ways. The three most popular methods are configuring the user interface (after starting the portal the first time), using `portal-ext.properties`, or using the JNDI approach. The following section explains these approaches.

Note that whatever approach you choose, you must create a database with the needed encoding (UTF8 in most cases) and user credentials for database access before starting the configuration in Liferay. After the connectivity configuration, it is mandatory to restart the Liferay DXP application server to see the connectivity.

Connectivity with a database requires three things—database configuration, a database connector, and a database.

- **Database connectivity from the UI**: As you learned at the beginning of this section, the Liferay DXP portal cannot be started without database connectivity, and HSQL helps. Once the portal starts with HSQL, there is a screen on the browser to connect the database with your instance of Liferay. See Figure 2-4. Once configured, these configurations are stored in `portal-setup-wizard.properties`. This is the easiest way to connect to a database. However, this screen will not appear if connection details are provided elsewhere in the system.

DATABASE
―――

« Use Default Database

Database Type

| MySQL | ⇕ |

JDBC URL *

| jdbc:mysql://path-to-my-database/my-liferay-database?characterEncoding=UTF-8&dontTrackOpenRe |

JDBC Driver Class Name *

| com.mysql.cj.jdbc.Driver |

User Name

| |

Password

| |

SAMPLE DATA
―――

☐ Add Sample Data ❶

Finish Configuration

Figure 2-4. *Database connectivity using the UI*

- **Database connectivity from `portal-ext.properties`**:
  Connecting to the database using the properties file
  is a straightforward configuration approach. You
  can provide connectivity-related details in either of
  the `portal-ext.properties` files. This property file
  serves as a master resource bundle for most portal
  configurations. This uses the JDBC approach for
  connectivity. To connect, you must mention four
  properties and values, listed here:

`jdbc.default.driverClassName=` This property tells Liferay to load the respective driver while connecting to the database. It provides all the essential classes and interfaces to make pooled connections with databases. For example, to connect to MySQL 8, you use the `com.mysql.cj.jdbc.Driver` driver class.

`jdbc.default.url=` This is the connection URL. It contains the protocol, host, port number, database name, and other optional parameters such as encoding, and so on. The following example is a sample connection URL that connects to a MySQL 8 database:

`jdbc:mysql://localhost/lportal74?characterEn coding=UTF-8`

`jdbc.default.username=` This is a key to provide a username to authenticate the connection.

`jdbc.default.password=` This is a key to provide a password to authenticate the connection.

- **Database connectivity via JNDI**: This approach comes from traditional Java applications and is the most complicated among those mentioned. The Java Naming and Directory Interface (JNDI) is an application programming interface (API) that provides naming and directory functionality to Java applications. JNDI connectivity is generally preferred in production environments because of better garbage handling and multithreading, thus improved performance. To do connectivity, you must set the configurations in the following files—`context.xml` and `portal-ext.properties`—as explained in Listings 2-5 and 2-6.

Listing 2-5. Context.xml Configuration

```xml
<?xml version="1.0" encoding="UTF-8"?>

<Context>
        <WatchedResource>WEB-INF/web.xml</WatchedResource>
        <WatchedResource>WEB-INF/tomcat-web.xml
        </WatchedResource>
        <WatchedResource>${catalina.base}/conf/web.xml</
        WatchedResource>
        <ResourceLink name="jdbc/read/LiferayPool"
        global="jdbc/read/LiferayPool" type="javax.sql.
        DataSource"></ResourceLink>
        <ResourceLink name="jdbc/write/LiferayPool"
        global="jdbc/write/LiferayPool" type="javax.sql.
        DataSource"></ResourceLink>
        <ResourceLink name="jdbc/defaultPool" global="jdbc/
        defaultPool" type="javax.sql.DataSource"></
        ResourceLink>

</Context>
```

Listing 2-6. The portal-ext.properties File Configuration

```
web.server.protocol=https

##Entries for Clustering
jdbc.default.jndi.name=jdbc/write/LiferayPool

jdbc.read.jndi.name=jdbc/read/LiferayPool
jdbc.read.username=root
jdbc.read.username=DBpassword
```

```
jdbc.write.jndi.name=jdbc/write/LiferayPool
jdbc.write.username=root
jdbc.write.username=DBpassword

counter.jdbc.prefix=jdbc.write.
```

Once you're connected to the database, you will see connectivity confirmation logs, like those shown in Figure 2-5.

```
.iferay 7.x at localhost [Liferay 7.x] C:\Program Files\Java\jdk1.8.0_181\bin\javaw.exe (20-Mar-2022, 10:20:36 pm)
20-Mar-2022 16:50:40.147 INFO [main] org.apache.catalina.startup.Catalina.load Server initialization in [1159] milliseconds
Loading jar:file:/C:/'    ''   /book/liferay-dxp-7.4.13-ga1/tomcat-9.0.53/webapps/ROOT/WEB-INF/shielded-container-lib/portal-impl.jar!/
Loading jar:file:/C:/  ....../book/liferay-dxp-7.4.13-ga1/tomcat-9.0.53/webapps/ROOT/WEB-INF/shielded-container-lib/portal-impl.jar!/
Loading file:/C:/'    ''   /book/liferay-dxp-7.4.13-ga1/portal-ext.properties
Loading file:/C:/'    ''   /book/liferay-dxp-7.4.13-ga1/tomcat-9.0.53/webapps/ROOT/WEB-INF/classes/portal-developer.properties
Loading file:/C:/..........book/liferay-dxp-7.4.13-ga1/portal-setup-wizard.properties
2022-03-20 16:50:45.543 INFO  [main][PortalContextLoaderListener:123] JVM arguments: -Dcatalina.base=C:/Schneider/book/liferay-dxp-7.4
Sun Mar 20 16:50:53 GMT 2022 WARN: Establishing SSL connection without server's identity verification is not recommended. According to
Sun Mar 20 16:50:53 GMT 2022 WARN: Establishing SSL connection without server's identity verification is not recommended. According to
Sun Mar 20 16:50:53 GMT 2022 WARN: Establishing SSL connection without server's identity verification is not recommended. According to
Sun Mar 20 16:50:53 GMT 2022 WARN: Establishing SSL connection without server's identity verification is not recommended. According to
Sun Mar 20 16:50:53 GMT 2022 WARN: Establishing SSL connection without server's identity verification is not recommended. According to
Sun Mar 20 16:50:53 GMT 2022 WARN: Establishing SSL connection without server's identity verification is not recommended. According to
Sun Mar 20 16:50:53 GMT 2022 WARN: Establishing SSL connection without server's identity verification is not recommended. According to
Sun Mar 20 16:50:53 GMT 2022 WARN: Establishing SSL connection without server's identity verification is not recommended. According to
Sun Mar 20 16:50:53 GMT 2022 WARN: Establishing SSL connection without server's identity verification is not recommended. According to
Sun Mar 20 16:50:53 GMT 2022 WARN: Establishing SSL connection without server's identity verification is not recommended. According to
2022-03-20 16:50:53.897 INFO  [main][DialectDetector:149] Using dialect org.hibernate.dialect.MySQLDialect for MySQL 5.7
Sun Mar 20 16:50:57 GMT 2022 WARN: Establishing SSL connection without server's identity verification is not recommended. According to
Sun Mar 20 16:50:58 GMT 2022 WARN: Establishing SSL connection without server's identity verification is not recommended. According to
Sun Mar 20 16:50:58 GMT 2022 WARN: Establishing SSL connection without server's identity verification is not recommended. According to
Sun Mar 20 16:50:58 GMT 2022 WARN: Establishing SSL connection without server's identity verification is not recommended. According to
Sun Mar 20 16:50:58 GMT 2022 WARN: Establishing SSL connection without server's identity verification is not recommended. According to
Sun Mar 20 16:50:58 GMT 2022 WARN: Establishing SSL connection without server's identity verification is not recommended. According to
Sun Mar 20 16:50:58 GMT 2022 WARN: Establishing SSL connection without server's identity verification is not recommended. According to
Sun Mar 20 16:50:58 GMT 2022 WARN: Establishing SSL connection without server's identity verification is not recommended. According to
2022-03-20 16:50:58.553 INFO  [main][ModuleFrameworkImpl:1272] Starting initial bundles
2022-03-20 16:51:03.905 INFO  [main][ModuleFrameworkImpl:1569] Started initial bundles
2022-03-20 16:51:03.905 INFO  [main][ModuleFrameworkImpl:1618] Starting dynamic bundles
2022-03-20 16:51:36.705 INFO  [main][ModuleFrameworkImpl:1640] Started dynamic bundles
2022-03-20 16:51:36.706 INFO  [main][ModuleFrameworkImpl:1647] Starting web bundles
```

Figure 2-5. *Database connectivity via the JNDI connection log*

This section has explained how to connect Liferay DXP to the database; in the next section, you are introduced to the Gogo shell.

Gogo Shell

The Gogo shell is the command-line interface for OSGi and was developed by the Apache Organization. Its full name is Apache Felix Gogo Shell and it's a subproject of Apache Felix implementation. It is very generic and is used in various servers and runtime environments such as Eclipse IDE,

Apache Karaf, and so on. As Liferay Developer Studio uses Eclipse as a base; it is very well used there as well.

Felix Gogo shell is available in three bundles. These three bundles are the building blocks of Gogo shell availability in the OSGi container:

- Command: Gogo shell commands are part of the Org. apache.felix.gogo.command package, and they contain a set of basic commands.

- Runtime: The Gogo shell runtime is included in the Org.apache.felix.gogo.runtime package and is the backbone of command-processing ability.

- Shell: Gogo shell is present in the Org.apache. felix.gogo.shell package and is responsible for the command-line interface.

The Gogo shell is very similar to the UNIX Bash shell, but with the following differences:

- It is for the OSGi framework,

- Unlike the UNIX Bash, it converts all arguments to strings,

- All the public methods are used as command names to operate on data and objects,

The Gogo shell used in Liferay DXP allows you to use all Felix Gogo shell basic commands and Liferay commands. Also, in Liferay DXP, the Gogo shell can be accessed from the Liferay DXP Control Panel, the Blade CLI, and telnet. However, Liferay recommends using it from the control panel. You must make sure the application server is up and running. Gogo shell is excellent for managing OSGi bundle lifecycles using commands. You have already seen the bundle states, and those states can be changed from the Gogo shell using various commands, including install, start, stop, and so on. This is how the modularity of Liferay DXP comes into action.

You will see the Gogo shell in action in the next chapter. Here, you see how it looks on the terminal to give you an overview. Figure 2-6 shows the list of available bundles with different server states. I hope this is enough to make you interested and want to experiment with the Gogo shell.

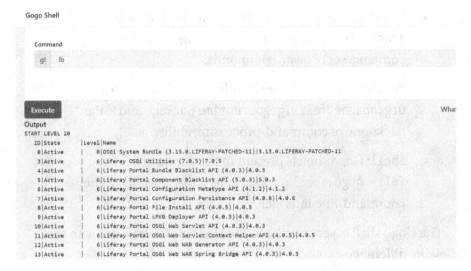

Figure 2-6. *The Gogo shell's Installed bundles list*

Summary

In this chapter, you learned how to leverage the power of the Liferay workspace for setting up development environments and their fundamental parts. Next, you learned how to build modules using Gradle and Maven. Once you were familiar with the Liferay workspace, you learned how to create a Liferay module. Further, you learned how to start the Liferay DXP server and connect your Liferay DXP instance to the database. Lastly, you were introduced to the Blade CLI and Gogo shell.

CHAPTER 3

Portlet Module Development

Portlets are the body and soul of any portal system and Liferay DXP is no different. Without a portlet, custom functionalities cannot be added to any portal. The Liferay portlet enables you to utilize features defined in the portlet specifications, and the cherries on top are the additional features Liferay provides to maximize the utilization of the framework. LiferayMVC is the most implemented portlet type and provides a lot of flexibility to developers. In this chapter, you get some hands-on experience with portlet development basics.

Introduction to Portlets

A *portlet* is nothing but a web component that is reusable and consists of a view (HTML/JSP page) and a controller (in Liferay, it's called a *controller class*). A portlet can also have a model (in the form of classes), which is used when you connect the portlet to a database table. The model, view, and controller working together act as a web component, which can process a login to the controller and model classes and can send information to the portlet's UI. However, you don't always need a controller and model in a portlet; a static portlet can also render an HTML/JSP page.

© Apoorva Prakash and Shaik Inthiyaz Basha 2022
A. Prakash and S. I. Basha, *Hands- On Liferay DXP*,
https://doi.org/10.1007/978-1-4842-8563-3_3

Without portlets, you have minimal information on the page, i.e., the header, footer, and navigation menu. To show information on a page and to add dynamic capability, you need to add portlets. Administrators can add these portlets to a page by simple drag-and-drop techniques. You can see this with the sample layout shown in Figure 3-1.

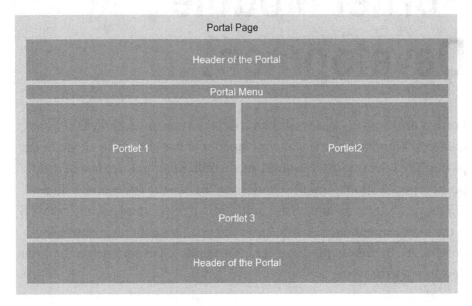

Figure 3-1. *Portal page layout view*

Figure 3-1 shows a sample page where the header and footer of the portal are static, and three portlets are added to the page. This is an example; you can have as many portlets as needed on a single page.

A single portlet can be added more than once; these are called *instantiable portlets*. Portlets can also communicate with each other. This mechanism is called *inter-portlet communication* (IPC). The display part of the portlets is highly customizable using CSS, and client-side dynamic functionalities can also be added using JavaScript and jQuery.

To summarize, portlets provide a means of presenting data from one or more sources in a manageable way. A portlet forms a section of the page to be rendered to the end user, making it very useful because several different portlets can be placed on a single page. The end user gets an immersive experience on a single page, whereas it is being rendered separately and from multiple sources.

This section has explained portlet basics; in the next section, you learn about portlet specifications.

Portlet Specifications

Portals and portlets have standards, which essentially define their behavior across all available and upcoming platforms. The first set of standards was introduced in 2003, called the Java Portlet Specification 1.0 or JSR-168. The second set of standards was published in 2008 and was referred to as the Java Portlet Specification 2.0, or JSR-286. The 2.0 specifications were processed on the foundation of JSR-168. JSR-286 ensured backward compatibility while introducing new features, such as inter-portlet communication (IPC), filters and listeners, and more. The latest Java Portlet Specification—3.0 (JSR-362)—was introduced in 2017. It continues the evolution and has added features such as resource dependencies and the Explicit Render state. We do not go into detail about these specifications as they are worthy of a separate book, but if you're interested, you can read about them on the web in detail.

This section has explained the basics of portlet specifications; in the next section, you learn about the portlet lifecycle.

Portlet Lifecycle

As the name suggests, a lifecycle represents the transition of state of anything, and it is no different in the case of a portlet. A portlet instance changes various states, from initialization and destruction, and this is referred to as the portlet lifecycle. The portlet container manages the state transition, which in this case is Liferay DXP portal. Oftentimes, people confuse servlet lifecycles with servlets, but there are significant differences between them. A portlet needs a portlet container just like a servlet requires a servlet container. A servlet container has three states— init(), service(), and destroy(). Similarly, a portlet lifecycle has the following stages:

- init(): This is the first stage of the portlet lifecycle and is invoked by the portlet container when it is needed to initialize the portlet. The init() method is used for the same. A portlet is initialized only when deployed in the portlet container; the container destroys the existing portlet (if any are available), and then init() is called to initialize it.

- render(): Once the portlet is deployed and initialized, it is ready to be added it to the page. When it is added to the page, the default UI of the portlet is rendered for the end user. To render the default view (or any view per se), render() is invoked. Internally, this method will process the configured HTML/JSP and return the HTML content to the portlet for showing the UI to the end user.

- processAction: This method is invoked when the Action URL is used in a portlet. As the name suggests, this is used to process any action for the end user, such as clicking a button or hyperlink, and generally, these actions are CRUD operations.

- processEvent(): This method was introduced in the Portlet Specifications 2.0 (JSR 286). This is mainly used for inter-portlet communication, also introduced in the same JSR 286 standards. This method is invoked on an event raised by another portlet. You learn more about IPC in a later part of the book.

- serveResource(): This method was also introduced in the Portlet Specifications 2.0 (JSR 286) and is used for AJAX request handling. It is invoked when a Liferay resource URL is processed.

- destroy(): This is the last method of a portlet lifecycle and is executed when the portlet is undeployed from the portlet container. This method ensures that the portlet is removed from the portlet container and is no longer available on the portal so cannot be added to the page.

Figure 3-2 shows the portlet lifecycle graphically.

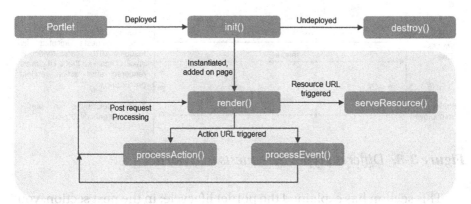

Figure 3-2. *Portlet lifecycle*

Figure 3-3 shows the flow within a portlet and several types of requests.

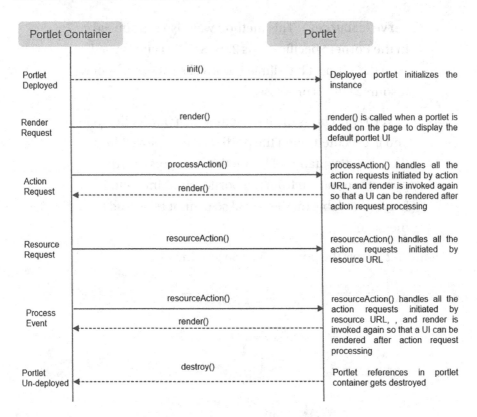

Figure 3-3. *Different types of requests in a portlet*

This section has explained the portlet lifecycle; in the next section, you learn about portlet modes and window states.

Portlet Modes and Window States

Another difference portlets have from servlets is portlet modes, which are distinct modes and window states.

Portlet Mode

The portlet mode of a portlet helps identify its function so that it can render different content based on the actions they perform. These portlets have dedicated features provided in different portlet modes to enhance accessibility. Each defined portlet mode must have a controller class and view. There are three main portlet modes:

- **View mode**: This is the default mode of any portlet and is the most commonly used mode. This mode is used to access the portlet's default/main functionality.

- **Edit mode**: This is a portlet's configuration mode used to customize the portlet's default view or behavior. You can use this mode when you want to let users perform actions in Edit mode so that customization can be done.

- **Help mode**: This mode provides helpful information to the end users.

Liferay DXP also has a few additional window states—About, Config, Edit Default, Edit Guest, Print, and Preview Mode.

Window States

A portlet window state is a way to control the area of space that a portlet takes up on a page. An easy way to understand this is to consider how you can resize, maximize, minimize, and restore an Explorer window in Microsoft Windows, assuming each state can have a different display view attached to it. The JSR Portlet Specification Standard mentions three portlet states; however, Liferay provides additional window states for more flexibility:

- **Normal Window State**: This is the default window state of a portlet and allows a portlet to be present with other visible portlets on the same page.

- **Maximized Window State**: This window state is rendered; when it expands on a complete page of the portal, other portlets are not rendered, and only the portlet in a maximized window state is visible on the entire page.

- **Minimized Window State**: This allows only the title bar of the portlet to be visible on the page.

This section has explained portlet modes and window states; in the next section, you learn the basics of Java standard portlets.

Java Standard Portlets

Java standard portlets are nothing but portlets made with JSR standards. These standard portlets are also referred to as generic portlets. The GenericPortlet class (`javax.portlet.GenericPortlet`) provides the default implementation for the portlet interface; an abstract class to be subclassed to create portlets. It is mandatory for a GenericPortlet subclass to use either an annotation or to override at least one method. Possible annotations or methods to override can be one of the following:

- **Annotation**: `@ProcessAction`, `@ProcessEvent`, and `@RenderMode`

- **Methods to override**: `processAction`, `doView`, `doEdit`, `doHelp`, `init`, and `destroy`

Listing 3-1 shows a Java standard portlet. It is extending GenericPortlet by overriding all its default methods. This example counts the render and action requests of a portlet with the help of two customized methods.

Listing 3-1. HelloApressPortlet Class Extending GenericPortlet

```java
package com.apress.handsonliferay.portlet;

import java.io.IOException;

import javax.portlet.ActionRequest;
import javax.portlet.ActionResponse;
import javax.portlet.EventRequest;
import javax.portlet.EventResponse;
import javax.portlet.GenericPortlet;
import javax.portlet.PortletException;
import javax.portlet.RenderRequest;
import javax.portlet.RenderResponse;

public class HelloApressPortlet extends GenericPortlet {

        private static int myRenderCount = 0;
        private static int myActionCount = 0;

        @Override
        public void render(RenderRequest request,
        RenderResponse response) throws PortletException,
        IOException {
                synchronized (this) {
                        myRenderCount++;
                }
                response.getWriter().print("<form
                action="+response.createActionURL()+">"
                        +"<p> Show the Render Count
                        <b>"+myRenderCount+"</b></p>"
                        +"<p> Show the Action Count
                        <b>"+myActionCount+"</b></p>"
```

```java
                                +"<input type='submit'/></
                                form>");
    }
    @Override
    public void processAction(ActionRequest request,
    ActionResponse response) throws PortletException,
    IOException {
            synchronized (this) {
                    myActionCount++;
            }
    }
    @Override
    public void processEvent(EventRequest request,
    EventResponse response) throws PortletException,
    IOException {
            // TODO Auto-generated method stub
            super.processEvent(request, response);
    }
    @Override
    protected void doView(RenderRequest request,
    RenderResponse response) throws PortletException,
    IOException {
            // TODO Auto-generated method stub
            super.doView(request, response);
    }
    @Override
    protected void doEdit(RenderRequest request,
    RenderResponse response) throws PortletException,
    IOException {
            // TODO Auto-generated method stub
            super.doEdit(request, response);
    }
```

```
@Override
protected void doHelp(RenderRequest request,
RenderResponse response) throws PortletException,
IOException {
        // TODO Auto-generated method stub
        super.doHelp(request, response);
}
@Override
public void init() throws PortletException {
        // TODO Auto-generated method stub
        super.init();
}
}
```

In this example, if you observed the render method, you created an ActionURL using the createActionURL method. These URLs are called portlet URLs. In the example, a portlet URL will reference the instance of the portlet in the portal page. (There will be different PortletURLs even if the same portlet class is being used in more than one portlet.)

The portlet creates PortletURL objects that represent portlet URLs. The portlet itself can use one of two methods on the RenderResponse class to create these PortletURL objects. The portlet container is responsible for creating these URLs, as it parsed the portlet URL into parameters for the portlet request.

- createActionURL: This method creates the action URL for forms or links that will be used to process the actions on the portlets.

- createRenderURL: This method creates the render URLs for tasks that don't contain the portlet's state modifications.

You can also add `PortletURL` to your content with no parameters, and you can set your parameters on a `PortletURL` by invoking the following method.

```
setParameter(name, value)
```

A Closer Look at HelloApressPortlet

You learned about the other methods in the portlet lifecycle section. Notice that there are different types of requests/responses in Listing 3-1. This section discusses each request and response in detail:

- `RenderRequest`: Represents the request sent to the portlet to handle a render. The `RenderRequest` object is created by the portlet container and then is handed over to the portlet's `render()` method as an argument.

- `RenderResponse`: Defines an object to assist a portlet in sending a response to the portal. The `RenderResponse` object is created by the portlet container and then handed over to the portlet's `render()` method as an argument.

- `ActionRequest`: Represents the request sent to the portlet to handle an action. The `ActionRequest` object is created by the portlet container and then handed over to the portlet's `processAction()` method as an argument.

- `ActionResponse`: Represents the response for an action request. The `ActionResponse` object is created by the portlet container and then handed over to the portlet's `processAction()` method as an argument.

- EventRequest: Represents the request sent to the portlet to handle an event. It extends the PortletRequest interface to provide event request information to portlets.

- EventResponse: Represents the portlet response to an event request.

In the portlet specifications, you have some predefined constants for the portlet level resource bundle. Here are the details about those constants:

- javax.portlet.title: The title should be displayed in the title bar of this portlet. Only one title per locale is allowed. Note that this title may be overridden by the portal or programmatically by the portlet.

- javax.portlet.short-title: A short version of the title that may be used for devices with limited display capabilities. Only one short title per locale is permitted.

- javax.portlet.keywords: Keywords describing the functionality of the portlet. Portals that allow users to search for portlets based on keywords may use these keywords. Multiple keywords per locale are permitted, but must be separated by commas.

- javax.portlet.description: Description of the portlet.

- javax.portlet.display-name: Name under which this portlet is displayed, deployment time or to tools. The display name need not be unique.

- javax.portlet.app.custom-portletmode.<,name>. decoration-name: Decoration name for the portlet managed custom portlet mode.

This section has explained the basics of Java standard portlets; in the next section, you learn about the Liferay portlet module.

Liferay Portlet Module (MVC Portlet)

Model View Controller (MVC) patterns are one of the most common patterns for developing Web applications worldwide. The Liferay MVC portlet is an implementation for developing Liferay DXP portlets. You should have an idea about how MVC works in a portlet, which was explained at the beginning of this chapter.

Liferay MVC has benefits compared to the standard MVC pattern, the greatest of which is that it's lightweight, being an extension of `GenericPortlet`. It minimizes the effort of maintaining separate configuration files. In addition, it provides an empty portlet file and folder structure, saving effort in writing initialization code with predefined parameters as part of the boilerplate. You can also break down the controller class into separate commands depending on the phases. It abstracts a lot of complexity of portlet development and makes it easier for developers to implement features and operations.

Liferay MVC Layers and Modularity: In Liferay MVC, you have three different layers:

- **Model**: This layer holds the application data and logic for manipulation.

- **View**: This layer displays the data.

- **Controller**: This layer acts as a middleman in the MVC pattern. It passes the data between the View and Model layers.

Liferay commonly uses three kinds of modules:

- **API**: These modules define the interfaces.

- **Implementation**: These modules provide concrete classes that implement interfaces.

- **Client**: These modules consume the APIs.

Now you see how to create an example Liferay MVC portlet to better understand the Liferay MVC portlets.

Creating a Sample Liferay MVC Portlet

This section assumes that you already have a local setup for Liferay. If so, you can follow these steps:

1. **Liferay workspace**: Open your Liferay Developer Studio with a Liferay workspace. This example uses apress_ws as a Liferay DXP workspace. This workspace contains all the code from this book.

2. **Template selection**: Right-click the Liferay workspace as shown in Figure 3-4 and select Liferay Module Project as the module template.

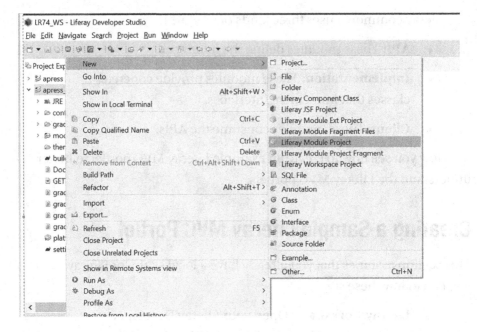

Figure 3-4. *Steps to create a Liferay module project*

In this example, we right-clicked the `apress_ws` workspace for module template selection.

3. **Create a Liferay module project**: After selecting a module template, you need to provide a project name. Name it `apressMVC` and then select Gradle for the build type and `mvc-portlet` for the project template name, as shown in Figure 3-5.

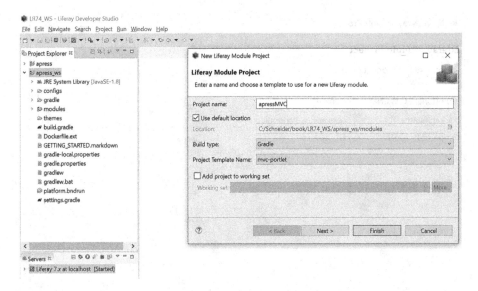

Figure 3-5. *Create the apressMVC portlet using Developer Studio*

Once you have selected Gradle for the build
type and `mvc-portlet` for the template, click the
Next button.

4. **Create a portlet**: Now, you need to provide your
    class name and package, or it will create one by
    default. Once you're done, click the Finish button.
    This example uses `ApressMVC` for the controller
    name and `com.apress.handsonliferay` for the
    package name, as shown in Figure 3-6.

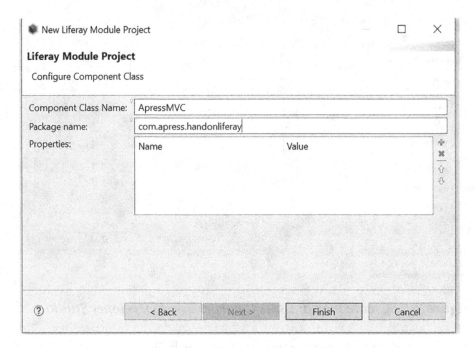

Figure 3-6. *Configure component class*

5. **ApressMVC portlet**: Once you click the Finish button, it will generate all required files for the Liferay MVC portlet with the default content from the template you selected.

6. **Portlet path**: This path will be created inside the modules folder of your workspace.

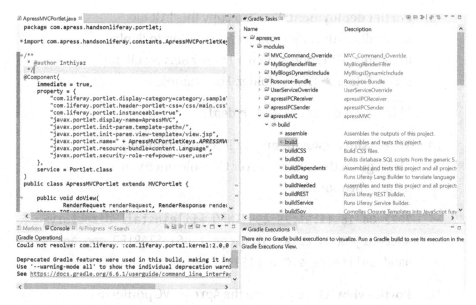

Figure 3-7. ApressMVC controller view in Developer Studio

7. **Portlet building**: As shown in Figure 3-7, you can see the Gradle Tasks window in the Liferay Developer Studio, which will help build the Liferay MVC portlet. Click the Build task by choosing Gradle Tasks ➤ apress_ws ➤ Modules ➤ apressMVC ➤ Build ➤ Build, as shown in Figure 3-7. This will build your Gradle module.

8. **Jar creation**: Once you click the Deploy task from Gradle Tasks ➤ apress_ws ➤ Modules ➤ apressMVC ➤ Build ➤ Deploy, it will generate the JAR file and store it in the workspace directory location apress_ws ➤ bundles ➤ osgi ➤ modules ➤ *.jar.

9. **Portlet deployment**: You can copy this JAR file manually to the following server location to deploy the ApressMVC portlet in the Liferay Server: Liferay server folder ➤ deploy folder. For example:

    `liferay-dxp-7.4.13-ga1 ➤deploy`

10. **Successful deployment**: You'll see the following message on the Liferay Server Console once you deploy the module.

    ```
    2022-04-18 11:51:25.495 INFO [fileinstall-directory-
    watcher][BundleStartStopLogger:46] STARTED com.apress.
    handsonliferay_1.0.0 [1535]
    ```

11. **Portlet view**: Once you add the `ApressMVC` portlet to your page, you'll see the output in Figure 3-8.

Figure 3-8. *Output of the ApressMVC portlet on a browser*

Understanding the Liferay MVC Portlet Controller

In this section, you learn more about the Liferay MVC portlet controller, which will be available for every MVC portlet. Let's look at the controller you created in the earlier example.

Note   All portlet customizations will be discussed based on the `ApressMVC` portlet created in the previous section.

The location of the controller is shown in Figure 3-9.

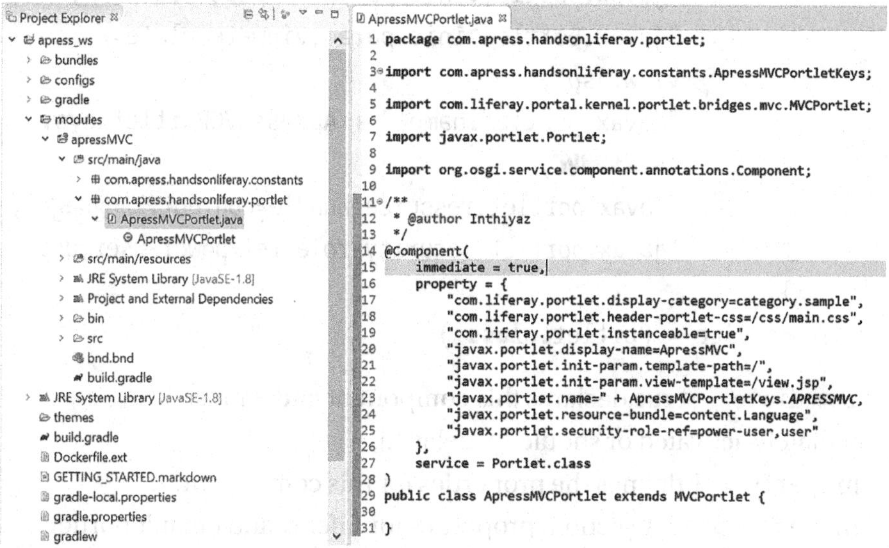

Figure 3-9. *Controller location in Developer Studio*

ApressMVCPortlet extends Liferay's MVCPortlet class from com.
liferay.portal.kernel.portlet.bridges.mvc.MVCPortlet, which
will help this class become the controller for the MVC pattern. In this
controller, the most important section is @Component.

Let's discuss @Component in detail, using the example shown in Listing 3-2.

Listing 3-2. Component Section in Controller

```
@Component(
        immediate = true,
        property = {
                "com.liferay.portlet.display-category=category.
                sample",
                "com.liferay.portlet.header-portlet-css=/css/
                main.css",
                "com.liferay.portlet.instanceable=true",
```

```
                     "javax.portlet.display-name=ApressMVC",
                     "javax.portlet.init-param.template-path=/",
                     "javax.portlet.init-param.view-template=/
                     view.jsp",
                     "javax.portlet.name=" + ApressMVCPortletKeys.
                     APRESSMVC,
                     "javax.portlet.resource-bundle=content.Language",
                     "javax.portlet.security-role-ref=power-user,user"
            },
            service = Portlet.class )
```

immediate = true declares this component and it must be immediately activated or should be delayed.

property = { defines the properties for this component.

In the @Component section, properties for Liferay and default portlet properties of the Java portlet have been defined:

com.liferay.portlet.display-category=category.sample is the category to show the portlet

com.liferay.portlet.header-portlet-css=/css/main.css is the path of the CSS files

com.liferay.portlet.instanceable=true is the instanceable configuration

javax.portlet.display-name=ApressMVC displays the name of the portlet

javax.portlet.init-param.template-path=/ is the template path

javax.portlet.init-param.view-template=/view.jsp is the path for the View modules

javax.portlet.name=" + ApressMVCPortletKeys.
APRESSMVC is the portlet name

javax.portlet.resource-bundle=content.
Language is the locale configuration

javax.portlet.security-role-ref=power-
user,user contains the roles for the portlet

service = defines the types under which to register this component as a service.

Understanding the Different URLs in the Liferay MVC Portlet

In the Liferay MVC portlet, you have three types of URLs:

- Render URL

- Action URL

- Resource URL

Each URL has its own features; let's discuss them in detail.

Render URL

If you want users to access different portlet views, you must implement navigation to them, and this can be achieved with the help of Render URLs. Figure 3-10 shows the RenderURL created in the ApressMVC portlet.

In the ApressMVC portlet, by default, two JSPs (init.jsp and view.jsp) are created while creating the ApressMVC portlet; you will create one more JSP called renderexample.jsp to perform navigation in the same path.

```
∨ 🗁 apress_ws
  > 🗁 bundles
  > 🗁 configs
  > 🗁 gradle
  ∨ 🗁 modules
    ∨ 🗁 apressMVC
      > 🗁 src/main/java
      ∨ 🗁 src/main/resources
        > 🗁 content
        ∨ 🗁 META-INF
          ∨ 🗁 resources
            > 🗁 css
              🗎 init.jsp
              🗎 renderexample.jsp
              🗎 view.jsp
```

Figure 3-10. *JSP file path for apressMVC Portlet*

1. The init.jsp page is created by default. The MVC portlet template will have all tag libraries declared that are required for the Liferay MVC portlet, as shown in Listing 3-3.

Listing 3-3. apressMVC Portlet init.jsp

```
<%@ taglib uri="http://java.sun.com/jsp/jstl/core" prefix="c" %>

<%@ taglib uri="http://java.sun.com/portlet_2_0"
prefix="portlet" %>

<%@ taglib uri="http://liferay.com/tld/aui" prefix="aui" %>
<%@ taglib uri="http://liferay.com/tld/portlet"
prefix="liferay-portlet" %>
<%@ taglib uri="http://liferay.com/tld/theme" prefix="liferay-
theme" %>
<%@ taglib uri="http://liferay.com/tld/ui"
prefix="liferay-ui" %>
```

```
<liferay-theme:defineObjects />

<portlet:defineObjects />
```

2. The view.jsp page is created by default by the MVC portlet template and it includes init.jsp to include the tag libraries. You wrote the logic for creating a Render URL, which will redirect to the render example JSP page using the following tag (see Listing 3-4).

```
<portlet:renderURL var="renderURL">
        <portlet:param name="mvcPath" value=
        "/renderexample.jsp" />
</portlet:renderURL>
```

Listing 3-4. JSP Code Snippet for Render URL

```
<%@ include file="/init.jsp" %>
<div style="padding: 15px">
        <h1><div style="color:blue"> Portlet URL's Section
        </div></h1>
        <portlet:renderURL var="renderURL">
                <portlet:param name="mvcPath" value="/
                renderexample.jsp" />
        </portlet:renderURL>
        <portlet:actionURL name="firstAction"
        var="actionURL" />
        <table>
          <tr>
            <th>Render URL</th>
            <th>Action URL</th>
            <th>Resource URL</th>
          </tr>
```

```
    <tr>
      <td><h4><a href="<%= renderURL %>">Go to Render
      Page</a></h4></td>
      <td></td>
      <td></td>
    </tr>
  </table>
</div>

<style>
    table{
      border: 2px solid green;
      border-collapse: collapse;
    }
    th, td {
      border: 2px dotted blue;
      border-collapse: collapse;
      padding: 10px;
    }
```

3. You will create the renderexample.jsp page in the same path, as shown in Figure 3-10. This page also includes init.jsp to include the tag libraries (see Listing 3-5).

```
<portlet:renderURL var="landingURL">
        <portlet:param name="mvcPath" value="/view.jsp" />
</portlet:renderURL>
```

Listing 3-5. apressMVC Portlet renderexample.jsp

```
<%@ include file="/init.jsp" %>

<portlet:renderURL var="landingURL">
        <portlet:param name="mvcPath" value="/view.jsp" />
</portlet:renderURL>
```

```
<div style="padding: 15px">
        <div style="color:green"><h1>Rendering Page of Apress
        MVC Portlet</h1></div>
        <p>
                <a href="<%= landingURL %>"><h3>Go to Landing
                Page</h3></a>
        </p>
</div>
```

4. The ApressMVCPortlet.java class acts as a
    controller, created by the default MVC portlet
    template. In the controller class, you will write
    the logic in Listing 3-6 for rendering. The render
    method will be overridden to use the path you click.

Listing 3-6. apressMVC Portlet Controller with Render Method

```
package com.apress.handsonliferay.portlet;

import javax.portlet.RenderRequest;
import javax.portlet.RenderResponse;
import com.liferay.portal.kernel.portlet.bridges.mvc.
MVCPortlet;
import org.osgi.service.component.annotations.Component;
/**
 * @author Inthiyaz
 */
@Component(
        immediate = true,
        property = {
                "com.liferay.portlet.display-category=category.
                sample",
                "com.liferay.portlet.header-portlet-css=/css/
                main.css",
```

```
                "com.liferay.portlet.instanceable=true",
                "javax.portlet.display-name=ApressMVC",
                "javax.portlet.init-param.template-path=/",
                "javax.portlet.init-param.view-template=/
                view.jsp",
                "javax.portlet.name=" + ApressMVCPortletKeys.
                APRESSMVC,
                "javax.portlet.resource-bundle=content.
                Language",
                "javax.portlet.security-role-ref=power-
                user,user"
        },
        service = Portlet.class
)
public class ApressMVCPortlet extends MVCPortlet {

        @Override
        public void render(RenderRequest renderRequest,
        RenderResponse renderResponse)
                        throws IOException, PortletException {
                // TODO Auto-generated method stub
                String mvcPath = renderRequest.getParameter("
                mvcPath");
                System.out.println("MVC Path "+mvcPath);
        }
}
```

5. Once you deploy the ApressMVC portlet, you can
   see the screens shown in Figures 3-11 and 3-12 as
   output. From Screen1, if you click Go to Render
   Page, it will show Screen2. If you click Go to Landing
   Page on Screen2, it will redirect to Screen1.

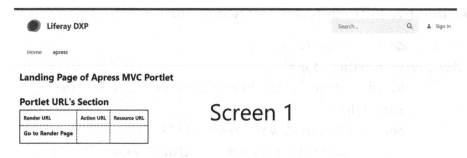

Figure 3-11. Output Screen1 for RenderURL execution

Figure 3-12. Output Screen2 for RenderURL execution

This example will help you navigate between Screen1 and Screen2 with the help of the Liferay MVC Portlet Render URL.

Action URL

This URL binds your portlets' action-handling methods to frontend/UI components using the portlet action URL. The following example helps elucidate the Action URL created in the ApressMVC portlet.

1. In the view.jsp file, you create the Action URLs in different ways available in Liferay MVC portlet, and these URL-related methods will be created in the controller of the ApressMVC portlet. The <portlet:actionURL> tag creates a URL, as shown in Listing 3-7.

Listing 3-7. JSP Code Snippet for Action URL

```jsp
<%@ include file="/init.jsp" %>
<div style="padding: 15px">
      <h1><div style="color:blue"> Portlet URL's Section
      </div></h1>
      <portlet:renderURL var="renderURL">
            <portlet:param name="mvcPath" value="/
            renderexample.jsp" />
      </portlet:renderURL>
      <portlet:actionURL name="firstAction" var="actionURL" />
      <table>
        <tr>
          <th>Render URL</th>
          <th>Action URL</th>
          <th>Resource URL</th>
        </tr>
        <tr>
          <td><h4><a href="<%= renderURL %>">Go to Render
          Page</a></h4></td>
          <td><h4><a href="<%= actionURL %>"><div style=
          "color:green">Test your First Action</div></a></h4>
              <h4><a href="<portlet:actionURL
              name="secondAction" />">Test your Second
              Action</a></h4>
              <h4><a href="<portlet:actionURL><portlet:param
              name="javax.portlet.action" value="nameForMoreA
              ctionsMethod" />
                    </portlet:actionURL>">
                          <div style="color:red">
                          Do Something More Actions
                          </div></a>
```

```
                    </h4></td>
        <td></td>
      </tr>
    </table>
</div>

<style>
    table{
      border: 2px solid green;
      border-collapse: collapse;
    }
    th, td {
      border: 2px dotted blue;
      border-collapse: collapse;
      padding: 10px;
    }
```

2. In the ApressMVCPortlet.java controller class, you write the following logic for all action methods that are created in the view.jsp file.To execute the action method, the name parameter value of <portlet:actionURL> in the JSP page and the action method name in ApressMVCPortlet should be the same, as shown here:

name=*"firstAction"* ➤ **public void** firstAction(

Listing 3-8 shows an example of this in action.

Listing 3-8. apressMVC Portlet Controller Code Snippet for Action Method

```
import org.osgi.service.component.annotations.Component;
/**
 * @author Inthiyaz
 */
@Component(
        immediate = true,
        property = {
                "com.liferay.portlet.display-category=category.
                sample",
                "com.liferay.portlet.header-portlet-css=/css/
                main.css",
                "com.liferay.portlet.instanceable=true",
                "javax.portlet.display-name=ApressMVC",
                "javax.portlet.init-param.template-path=/",
                "javax.portlet.init-param.view-template=/
                view.jsp",
                "javax.portlet.name=" + ApressMVCPortletKeys.
                APRESSMVC,
                "javax.portlet.resource-bundle=content.
                Language",
                "javax.portlet.security-role-ref=power-
                user,user"
        },
        service = Portlet.class
)
public class ApressMVCPortlet extends MVCPortlet {

        public void firstAction(
                        ActionRequest actionRequest,
                        ActionResponse actionResponse) {
```

```
            System.out.println("Invoking first Action");
    }
    public void secondAction(
                    ActionRequest actionRequest,
                    ActionResponse actionResponse) {

            System.out.println("Invoking second Action");
    }

    @ProcessAction(name = "nameForMoreActionsMethod")
    public void moreActionsMethod(
                    ActionRequest actionRequest,
                    ActionResponse actionResponse) {
            System.out.println("Invoking
            nameForMoreActionsMethod ");

    }
}
```

3. Once you deploy the ApressMVC portlet, you will
   see the screen in Figure 3-13 as output. If you click
   any action URL that you created in JSP, you'll see a
   message in the Liferay Server Console.

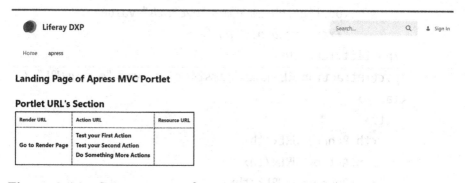

Figure 3-13. *Output screen for Action URL*

Resource URL

This URL performs tasks without refreshing your page. The best example for this URL is the auto-complete feature in Google search (it will fetch the matching result while typing itself). The following example explains the ResourceURL, created in the ApressMVC portlet. In this example, try downloading a sample file called apressMVCResource.csv using the Resource function.

1. In the View.jsp page, you are creating the ResourceURL to call the Resource method of the controller. <portlet:ResourceURL> creates the resource URL, which calls the serveResource method of the controller. Listing 3-9 illustrates this process.

Listing 3-9. JSP Code Snippet for the Resource URL

```
<%@ include file="/init.jsp" %>
<div style="padding: 15px">
        <h1><div style="color:blue"> Portlet URL's Section
        </div></h1>
        <portlet:renderURL var="renderURL">
                <portlet:param name="mvcPath" value=
                "/renderexample.jsp" />
        </portlet:renderURL>
        <portlet:actionURL name="firstAction" var="actionURL" />
        <table>
          <tr>
            <th>Render URL</th>
            <th>Action URL</th>
            <th>Resource URL</th>
          </tr>
```

```html
<tr>
  <td><h4><a href="<%= renderURL %>">Go to Render
  Page</a></h4></td>
  <td><h4><a href="<%= actionURL %>"><div style=
  "color:green">Test your First Action</div></a></h4>
      <h4><a href="<portlet:actionURL name=
      "secondAction" />">Test your Second
      Action</a></h4>
      <h4><a href="<portlet:actionURL><portlet:param
      name="javax.portlet.action" value="nameForMoreA
      ctionsMethod" />
              </portlet:actionURL>">
                      <div style="color:red">Do
                      Something More Actions</div></a>
              </h4></td>
  <td><h4><a href="<portlet:resourceURL
  id="resourceURL" />"><div style="color:green">
  Resource URL</div></a></h4></td>
  </tr>
</table>
</div>

<style>
    table{
       border: 2px solid green;
       border-collapse: collapse;
    }
    th, td {
       border: 2px dotted blue;
       border-collapse: collapse;
       padding: 10px;
    }
```

2. In the ApressMVCPortlet.java controller, you are overriding the serveResource method to write the logic to download a file called apressMVCResource. csv at every click of the ResourceURL from the JSP page. See Listing 3-10.

Listing 3-10. apressMVC Portlet Controller Code Snippet for Resource Method

```java
import org.osgi.service.component.annotations.Component;
/**
 * @author Inthiyaz
 */
@Component(
        immediate = true,
        property = {
                "com.liferay.portlet.display-category=category.
                sample",
                "com.liferay.portlet.header-portlet-css=/css/
                main.css",
                "com.liferay.portlet.instanceable=true",
                "javax.portlet.display-name=ApressMVC",
                "javax.portlet.init-param.template-path=/",
                "javax.portlet.init-param.view-template=/
                view.jsp",
                "javax.portlet.name=" + ApressMVCPortletKeys.
                APRESSMVC,
                "javax.portlet.resource-bundle=content.
                Language",
                "javax.portlet.security-role-ref=power-
                user,user"
        },
```

```
        service = Portlet.class
)
public class ApressMVCPortlet extends MVCPortlet {
        @Override
        public void serveResource(ResourceRequest
        resourceRequest, ResourceResponse resourceResponse)
                        throws IOException, PortletException {
                // TODO Auto-generated method stub
                        System.out.println("Invoking Resource
                        Method ");
                        resourceResponse.
                        setContentType("text/csv");
                        resourceResponse.
                        addProperty(HttpHeaders.CONTENT_
                        DISPOSITION,
                        "attachment;filename=apressMVCResour
                        ce.csv");
                        OutputStream out = resourceResponse.
                        getPortletOutputStream();
                        out.flush();
                        System.out.println("Resource File
                        Downloaded Successfully ");
        }
}
```

3. Once you deploy the ApressMVC portlet, you can see the screen shown in Figure 3-14 as output. If you click the Resource URL link, it will download the file called resourcefile.csv, as shown in Figure 3-14.

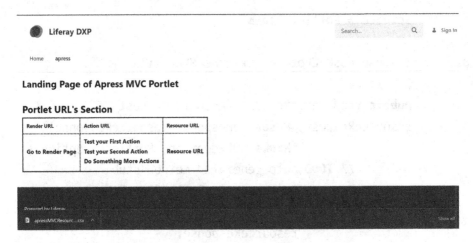

Figure 3-14. *Output screen for ResourceURL*

Understanding Different Commands in the Liferay MVC Portlet

This section explains the different commands available in Liferay MVC portlets.

- MVC Render command

- MVC Action command

- MVC Resource command

Each command has its own features; let's discuss each MVC command in detail.

The MVC Render Command

These classes handle which page to render, similar to other render methods. They are invoked by the `MVCPortlet` render URLs. If you want to build simple logic, you can implement all of it in your portlet class.

If you want to build complex logic, use the MVC Render commands. The following examples illustrate this concept. You'll be adding them to the ApressMVC portlet.

1. In the View.jsp page, you create the RenderURL to call the MVC Render command Class. The following tag is used to achieve that:

```
<portlet:renderURL var="renderCommandURL">
<portlet:param name="mvcRenderCommandName" value=
"/apressmvcrendercommand" />
</portlet:renderURL>
```

Listing 3-11 shows this process in action.

Listing 3-11. JSP Code Snippet with Render Command URL

```
<%@ include file="/init.jsp" %>
<div style="padding: 15px; color:green"><h1>Landing Page of
Apress MVC Portlet</h1></div>

<div style="padding: 15px">
        <h1><div style="color:blue"> MVC Command's Section
        </div></h1>
        <portlet:renderURL var="renderCommandURL">
                <portlet:param name="mvcRenderCommandName"
                value="/apressmvcrendercommand" />
        </portlet:renderURL>
        <table>
          <tr>
            <th>MVC Render Command</th>
            <th>MVC Action Command</th>
            <th>MVC Resource Command</th>
          </tr>
```

```
        <tr>
          <td><h3><a href="<%= renderCommandURL %>">Go to
          Render Command Page</a></h3></td>
          <td>

          </td>
          <td>

          </td>
        </tr>
      </table>
</div>
```

2. The apressmvcrendercommand.jsp file redirects
    from the MVC Render Command Class's render
    method whenever you click Go to Render
    Command Page from view.jsp. This JSP is created
    in the same path as view.jsp.

    ```
    <%@ include file="/init.jsp" %>
    ```

    ```
    <h1>Apress MVC Render Command Page</h1>
    ```

3. The ApressMVCRenderCommand.java class
    implements the logic for the MVC Render
    command. It will implement the MVCRenderCommand
    interface (com.liferay.portal.kernel.portlet.
    bridges.mvc.MVCRenderCommand) to achieve the
    MVC Render command features. This class is
    created in the path of ApressMVCPortlet.java. The
    following points are mandatory while implementing
    and will come in the Component section.

- service = MVCRenderCommand.class: The
  Component section

- "Javax.portlet.name=" + apressmvcportletkeys.
  APRESSMVC: The portlet name must be the same for your
  Render command class and MVC controller.

- mvc.command.name=/apressmvcrendercommand:
  This property value should be the same as your JSP
  <portlet:param name="mvcRenderCommandName"
  value="/apressmvcrendercommand" />.

  Listing 3-12 shows an example in action.

Listing 3-12. ApressMVCRenderCommand Class for the Render
Command URL

```
package com.apress.handsonliferay.portlet;

import com.apress.handsonliferay.constants.
ApressMVCPortletKeys;
import com.liferay.portal.kernel.portlet.bridges.mvc.
MVCRenderCommand;

import javax.portlet.PortletException;
import javax.portlet.RenderRequest;
import javax.portlet.RenderResponse;

import org.osgi.service.component.annotations.Component;

/**
 * @author Inthiyaz
 */
@Component(
        immediate = true,
        property = {
```

```
            "javax.portlet.name=" + ApressMVCPortletKeys.
            APRESSMVC,
            "mvc.command.name=/apressmvcrendercommand"
      },
      service = MVCRenderCommand.class
)
public class ApressMVCRenderCommand implements
MVCRenderCommand {

      @Override
      public String render(RenderRequest renderRequest,
      RenderResponse renderResponse) throws
      PortletException {
            System.out.println("Invoking Render Command
            Method ");
            return "/apressmvcrendercommand.jsp";
      }
}
```

4. Figure 3-15 shows the first screen that will display after deploying the ApressMVC portlet. If you click the Go to Render Command Page link from view.jsp, it will redirect to the screen shown in Figure 3-16 with the help of the Render method from the ApressMVCRenderCommand class.

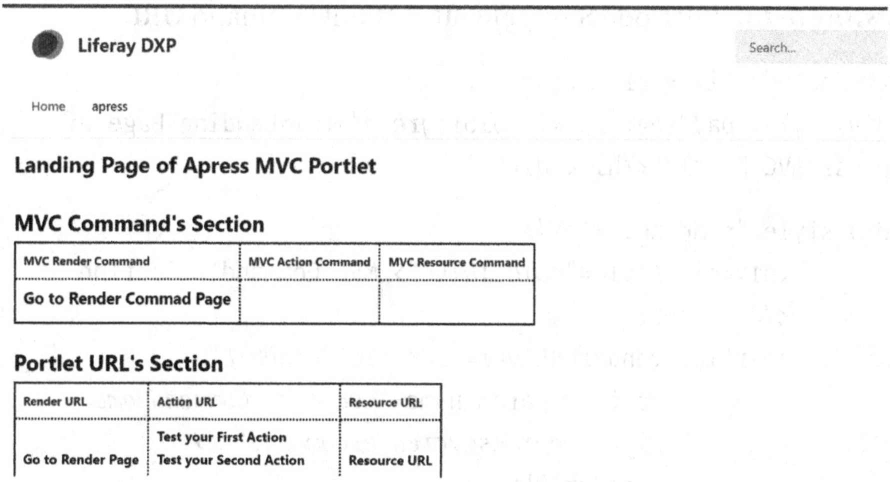

Figure 3-15. *Output screen with a Render Command link*

Figure 3-16. *Output screen for Render Command page*

MVC Action Command

This command handles actions as separate classes. With the help of Action commands, you can organize action logic in `MVCPortlet` that has many actions. These action URLs in the portlet's JSPs invoke a designated MVC Action command class. This section discusses in detail the MVC Action commands with an example.

1. In the `View.jsp` page, you create the Action URL to call the MVC Action command class by using the following tag:

    ```
    <portlet:actionURL name="/apressmvcactioncommand" />
    ```

Listing 3-13. JSP Code Snippet with ActionCommand URL

```
<%@ include file="/init.jsp" %>
<div style="padding: 15px; color:green"><h1>Landing Page of
Apress MVC Portlet</h1></div>

<div style="padding: 15px">
        <h1><div style="color:blue"> MVC Command's Section
        </div></h1>
        <portlet:renderURL var="renderCommandURL">
                <portlet:param name="mvcRenderCommandName"
                value="/apressmvcrendercommand" />
        </portlet:renderURL>
        <table>
          <tr>
            <th>MVC Render Command</th>
            <th>MVC Action Command</th>
            <th>MVC Resource Command</th>
          </tr>
          <tr>
            <td><h3><a href="<%= renderCommandURL %>">Go to
            Render Command Page</a></h3></td>
            <td>
                <h3><a href="<portlet:actionURL name="/
                apressmvcactioncommand" />">
                <div style="color:green"> Go to Action Command
                Class</div></a>
                </h3>
            </td>
            <td>
```

```
     </td>
    </tr>
   </table>
</div>
```

2. The ApressMVCActionCommand.java class
    implements the logic for the MVC Action command
    to execute the action methods. It will implement
    the MVCActionCommand interface, and this class is
    created in the ApressMVCPortlet.java path. The
    following points are mandatory while implementing
    and will be in the Component section.

    service = MVCActionCommand.**class**
    "javax.portlet.name=" + ApressMVCPortletKeys.***APRESSMVC***,

    The portlet name must be the same as your Action
    Command class and MVC Controller.

    The mvc.command.name=/apressmvcactioncommand
    command name from the Action command class must
    match the actionURL param of JSP <portlet:actionURL
    name="/apressmvcactioncommand" />. See Listing 3-14.

Listing 3-14. ApressMVCActionCommand Class for Action
Command URL

package com.apress.handsonliferay.portlet;

import com.apress.handsonliferay.constants.
ApressMVCPortletKeys;
import com.liferay.portal.kernel.portlet.bridges.mvc.
MVCActionCommand;

import javax.portlet.ActionRequest;
import javax.portlet.ActionResponse;
import javax.portlet.PortletException;

```java
import org.osgi.service.component.annotations.Component;

/**
 * @author Inthiyaz
 */
@Component(
        immediate = true,
        property = {
                "javax.portlet.name=" + ApressMVCPortletKeys.
                APRESSMVC,
                "mvc.command.name=/apressmvcactioncommand"
        },
        service = MVCActionCommand.class
)
public class ApressMVCActionCommand implements
MVCActionCommand {

        @Override
        public boolean processAction(ActionRequest
        actionRequest, ActionResponse actionResponse) throws
        PortletException {
                // TODO Auto-generated method stub
                System.out.println("Invoking Action Command
                Method ");
                return false;
        }
}
```

3. Figure 3-17 displays what you see after deploying
    the ApressMVC portlet. If you click the Go to Action
    command class, it will show the "Invoking Action
    Command Method" message in your Liferay
    Console.

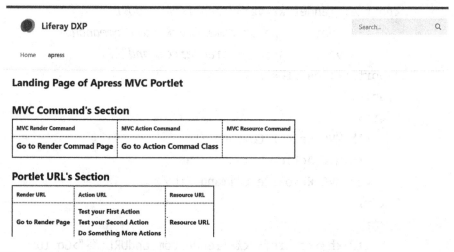

Figure 3-17. *Output screen with Action Command link*

MVC Resource Command

MVC Resource Command classes fetch resources such as XML, documents, images, or any other resources from a DXP/portal instance without triggering actions or renders. Requests or portlet resource URLs invoke MVC Resource commands. This section discusses in detail the MVC Resource commands with an example.

1. In the View.jsp page, you create the ResourceURL to call the MVC Resource command class.

```
<portlet:resourceURL id="/apressmvcresourcecommand" />
```

Listing 3-15. JSP Code Snippet with Resource Command URL

```
<%@ include file="/init.jsp" %>
<div style="padding: 15px; color:green"><h1>Landing Page of
Apress MVC Portlet</h1></div>

<div style="padding: 15px">
        <h1><div style="color:blue"> MVC Command's Section
        </div></h1>
```

```
<portlet:renderURL var="renderCommandURL">
        <portlet:param name="mvcRenderCommandName"
        value="/apressmvcrendercommand" />
</portlet:renderURL>
<table>
  <tr>
    <th>MVC Render Command</th>
    <th>MVC Action Command</th>
    <th>MVC Resource Command</th>
  </tr>
  <tr>
    <td><h3><a href="<%= renderCommandURL %>">Go to
    Render Command Page</a></h3></td>
    <td>
        <h3><a href="<portlet:actionURL name=
        "/apressmvcactioncommand" />">
        <div style="color:green"> Go to Action Command
        Class</div></a>
        </h3>
    </td>
    <td>
        <h3><a href="<portlet:resourceURL id="/
        apressmvcresourcecommand" />">
        <div style="color:red"> Resource Command URL to
        Download File </div></a>
        </h3>
    </td>
  </tr>
</table>
</div>
```

2. The ApressMVCResourceCommand.java class
    implements the logic for the MVC Resource
    command to execute the file download. It will
    implement the MVCResourceCommand interface, and
    this class is created in the ApressMVCPortlet.java
    path. The following points are mandatory while
    implementing and will come in the Component
    section.

    ```
    service = MVCResourceCommand.class
    "javax.portlet.name=" + ApressMVCPortletKeys.APRESSMVC,
    ```

    The portlet name must be the same as your resource
    command class and MVC controller.

    ```
    mvc.command.name=/apressmvcresourcecommand
    ```
    command name from the resource command
    class must match the resourceURL param
    of JSP <portlet:actionURL name="/
    apressmvcresourcecommand" />

Listing 3-16. ApressMVCResourceCommand with MVC Resource
Command Code Snippet

```java
package com.apress.handsonliferay.portlet;

import com.apress.handsonliferay.constants.ApressMVCPortletKeys;
import com.liferay.portal.kernel.portlet.bridges.mvc.
MVCResourceCommand;
import com.liferay.portal.kernel.servlet.HttpHeaders;

import java.io.IOException;
import java.io.OutputStream;
```

```java
import javax.portlet.PortletException;
import javax.portlet.ResourceRequest;
import javax.portlet.ResourceResponse;

import org.osgi.service.component.annotations.Component;

/**
 * @author Inthiyaz
 */
@Component(
        immediate = true,
        property = {
                "javax.portlet.name=" + ApressMVCPortletKeys.
                APRESSMVC,
                "mvc.command.name=/apressmvcresourcecommand"
        },
        service = MVCResourceCommand.class
)
public class ApressMVCResourceCommand implements
MVCResourceCommand {

        @Override
        public boolean serveResource(ResourceRequest
        resourceRequest, ResourceResponse resourceResponse)
                        throws PortletException {
                System.out.println("Invoking Resource
                Method ");
                  resourceResponse.setContentType("text/csv");
                  resourceResponse.addProperty
                  (HttpHeaders.CONTENT_DISPOSITION,
                      "attachment;filename=apressMVCResourceCom
                      mandFile.csv");
                  OutputStream out;
```

```
try {
        out = resourceResponse.
        getPortletOutputStream();
        out.flush();
} catch (IOException e) {
        // TODO Auto-generated catch block
        e.printStackTrace();
}

return false;
    }
}
```

3. If you click the Resource command URL
   to download a file after deploying the
   ApressMVC portlet, it will download a file called
   apressMVCResourceCommandFile.csv, as shown in
   Figure 3-18.

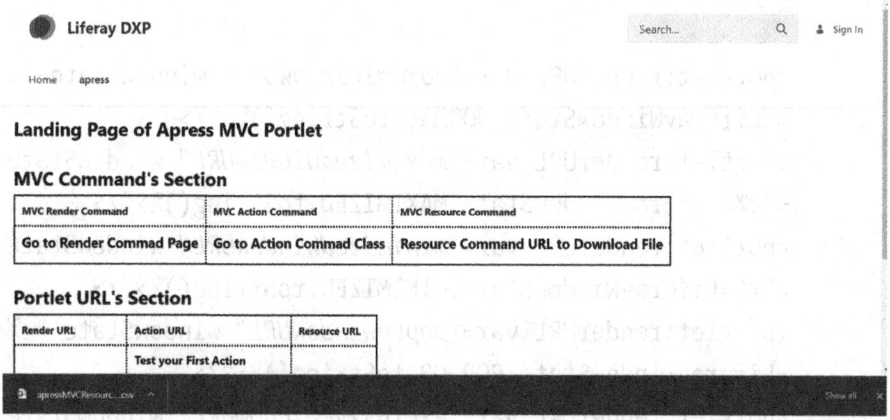

Figure 3-18. *Output screen with resource link and file download*

Implementing Window State

You have already read about the Window state in a previous section of this chapter. You will now try to implement it in your ApressMVC portlet by following these steps.

1. In the View.jsp page, you are creating the all window state URLs to execute; see Listing 3-17.

Listing 3-17. JSP Code Snippet for Window Modes

```
<%@ include file="/init.jsp" %>
<div style="padding: 15px; color:green"><h1>Landing Page of
Apress MVC Portlet</h1></div>

<div style="padding: 15px">
      <h1><div style="color:blue"> Portlet Mode example
      Section </div></h1>

      <%@page import="com.liferay.portal.kernel.portlet.
      LiferayWindowState"%>

      <portlet:renderURL var="normalWindowURL" windowState="<
      %=LiferayWindowState.NORMAL.toString()%>"/>
      <portlet:renderURL var="maximizedWindowURL" windowState
      ="<%=LiferayWindowState.MAXIMIZED.toString()%>"/>
      <portlet:renderURL var="minimizedWindowURL" windowState
      ="<%=LiferayWindowState.MINIMIZED.toString()%>"/>
      <portlet:renderURL var="popupWindowURL" windowState="<%
      =LiferayWindowState.POP_UP.toString()%>"/>
      <portlet:renderURL var="exclusiveWindowURL" windowState
      ="<%=LiferayWindowState.EXCLUSIVE.toString()%>"/>
      <table>
        <tr>
```

```
        <th>Normal Window</th>
        <th>Maximized Window</th>
        <th>Minimized Window</th>
        <th>Pop Up Window</th>
        <th>Exclusive View Window</th>
    </tr>
    <tr>
        <td><a href="<%=normalWindowURL.toString() %>">
        normalWindowURL now</a></td>
        <td><a href="<%=maximizedWindowURL.toString() %>">
        maximizedWindowURL now</a></td>
        <td><a href="<%=minimizedWindowURL.toString() %>">
        minimizedWindowURL now</a></td>
        <td><a href="<%=popupWindowURL.toString() %>">
        popupWindowURL now</a></td>
        <td><a href="<%=exclusiveWindowURL.toString() %>">
        exclusiveWindowURL now</a></td>
    </tr>
    </table>
</div>
```

2. Figure 3-19 shows the output screen that will display
    after you deploy the ApressMVC portlet with window
    states to the Liferay Server.

Landing Page of Apress MVC Portlet

Portlet Mode example Section

Normal Window	Maximized Window	Minimized Window	Pop Up Window	Exclusive View Window
normalWindowURL now	maximizedWindowURL now	minimizedWindowURL now	popupWindowURL now	exclusiveWindowURL now

MVC Command's Section

MVC Render Command	MVC Action Command	MVC Resource Command
Go to Render Commad Page	Go to Action Commad Class	Resource Command URL to Download File

Figure 3-19. *Output screen with a different Window mode link*

After every click, it will perform some actions.

This section has explained the Liferay portlet module; in the next section, you are introduced to other portlet modules that can be created in Liferay DXP.

Introduction to Other Portlet Modules

The Spring MVC Portlet

The next most popular portlet type in portlet development is the Spring MVC portlet. Liferay allows you to create/deploy portlets with the Spring framework. Liferay provides development standards, and any module that follows the standard is deployable in Liferay. This does not mean that other Liferay features, such as service builder, externalization, and so on, become useless if you are not using the Liferay MVC portlet. They are also usable in the Spring MVC portlet because it is essentially just a change in the application layer. PortletMVC4Spring is a way to develop portlets using the Spring Framework and the Model View Controller (MVC) pattern.

A significant difference between the Liferay MVC Portlet and the Spring MVC Portlet is that, when built for deployment, a Spring MVC module generates a WAR file instead of a JAR file. This is because it has become a Java EE-style web application. Thanks to Liferay for using OSGi WAB standards (Web Application Bundler) for deployment, you can deploy this WAR on the Liferay Server.

Liferay Soy Portlet

Liferay Soy portlet is essentially a Liferay MVC portlet with the added functionality of using Soy templates. Soy templates make it easy to create complex frontends.

JSF Portlet

Liferay provides support for JavaServer Faces standards. This is made possible with the help of the Liferay Faces Bridge. Liferay has created a separate project for supporting JSF named Liferay Faces. This Liferay Faces Bridge allows for the deployment of JSF applications, and the most significant advantage is that you need not write custom Java code. This is made possible with the support of JSF 2.0 standards within Liferay DXP. Other portlets supported by Liferay faces include Liferay Faces Alloy and Liferay Faces Portal.

Bean Portlet

Contexts and Dependency Injection (CDI) is part of the Portlet Specification 3.0, and Liferay supports this with the help of the Bean portlet. The Bean portlet allows custom CDI such as @PortletSessionScoped, @PortletRequestScoped, and @RenderStateScoped. CDI enables portlet classes instantiated via a CDI container, enabling dependency injection along with scope annotations of the portlet classes. Bean portlets are essentially just plain old Java objects (POJOs); descriptors mark them as portlets.

This section introduced different types of portlets; in the next section, you see the Gogo shell in action.

Gogo Shell in Action

From the explanation and example in the previous chapter, you know what the Gogo shell is and what it is capable of. Now you learn how you can use it in detail. Follows these steps to use the Gogo shell in Telnet.

To connect to the Gogo shell using Telnet, make sure:

- If you are using the Windows operating system, the Telnet feature is enabled in the Add/Remove programs section.

- If you are using Linux, Telnet should be installed.

To connect the Gogo shell using Telnet, you must also add the following properties to the `portal-ext.properties` file.

```
include-and-override=portal-developer.properties
```

You must use the following command:

```
telnet localhost 11311
```

where 11311 is the port number (default), which can be modified in `portal-ext.properties` using the following property:

```
module.framework.properties.osgi.console=11312
```

Once you execute this, you will get the screen with the g! prompt shown in Figure 3-20. Whoa! Welcome to the Gogo shell; you can execute commands now.

Figure 3-20. *Gogo shell command prompt screen*

Let's execute a command. Type **lb** and press Enter. You will see the list of available bundles and their states, as shown in Figure 3-21. The lb stands for list bundles. You may get 1,400+ bundles listed with this command.

```
Welcome to Apache Felix Gogo
g! lb
START LEVEL 20
   ID|State      |Level|Name
    0|Active     |    0|OSGi System Bundle (3.13.0.LIFERAY-PATCHED-11)|3.13.0.LIFERAY-PATCHED-11
    3|Active     |    6|Liferay OSGi Utilities (7.0.5)|7.0.5
    4|Active     |    6|Liferay Portal Bundle Blacklist API (4.0.3)|4.0.3
    5|Active     |    6|Liferay Portal Component Blacklist API (5.0.3)|5.0.3
    6|Active     |    6|Liferay Portal Configuration Metatype API (4.1.2)|4.1.2
    7|Active     |    6|Liferay Portal Configuration Persistence API (4.0.6)|4.0.6
    8|Active     |    6|Liferay Portal File Install API (4.0.5)|4.0.5
    9|Active     |    6|Liferay Portal LPKG Deployer API (4.0.3)|4.0.3
   10|Active     |    6|Liferay Portal OSGi Web Servlet API (4.0.3)|4.0.3
   11|Active     |    6|Liferay Portal OSGi Web Servlet Context Helper API (4.0.5)|4.0.5
   12|Active     |    6|Liferay Portal OSGi Web WAB Generator API (4.0.3)|4.0.3
   13|Active     |    6|Liferay Portal OSGi Web WAB Spring Bridge API (4.0.3)|4.0.3
   14|Active     |    6|Liferay Portal Profile API (5.0.6)|5.0.6
   15|Active     |    6|Liferay Portal Upgrade API (5.0.6)|5.0.6
   16|Active     |    6|Jackson-annotations (2.12.4)|2.12.4
   17|Active     |    6|Jackson-core (2.12.4)|2.12.4
   18|Active     |    6|jackson-databind (2.12.4)|2.12.4
   19|Active     |    6|Liferay OSGi Log Service Extender (5.0.5)|5.0.5
   20|Active     |    6|Liferay Portal Bundle Blacklist Implementation (4.0.9)|4.0.9
   21|Active     |    6|Liferay Portal Change Tracking (2.0.6)|2.0.6
   22|Active     |    6|Liferay Portal Class Loader Tracker (5.0.4)|5.0.4
   23|Active     |    6|Liferay Portal Component Blacklist Implementation (5.0.9)|5.0.9
   24|Active     |    6|Liferay Portal Configuration Persistence Implementation (4.0.6)|4.0.6
   25|Active     |    6|Liferay Portal Dependencymanager Component Executor Factory (3.0.5)|3.0.5
```

Figure 3-21. *Output of the lb command*

Let's try to start and stop a bundle using the start and stop commands. You can see in Figure 3-22 how to start and stop bundles from the Gogo shell prompt and how these commands reflect in the server logs in Figure 3-23.

Figure 3-22. *Output of the lb apress command*

Figure 3-23. *Output of the server logs of the start and stop commands*

To exit the Gogo shell, use the `disconnect` command. Quick tip: If you use Ctrl+C (Break), close, and exit either of the commands, it will shut down the OSGi container, which means your application server will be down. (See Figure 3-24.)

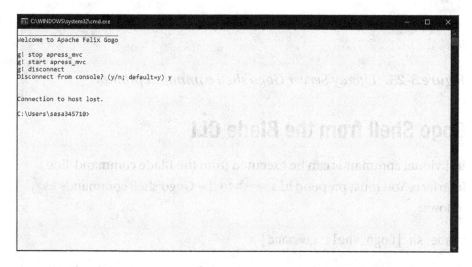

Figure 3-24. *Gogo shell command output for the start and stop commands*

Gogo Shell from the Liferay Control Panel

To access the Gogo shell from the control panel, choose Control Panel ➤ System ➤ Gogo Shell (see Figure 3-25).

The rest of the process remains the same as explained in the Gogo shell with Telnet section.

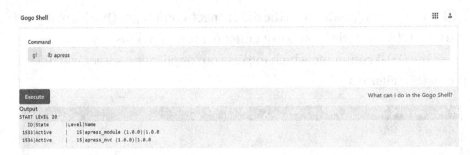

Figure 3-25. *Liferay Server Gogo shell command prompt*

Gogo Shell from the Blade CLI

Individual commands can be executed from the Blade command-line interface. You must prepend blade sh to the Gogo shell commands as follows:

blade sh [Gogo shell command]

The rest of the process remains exactly the same as explained in the Gogo shell with the Telnet section. (See Figure 3-26.)

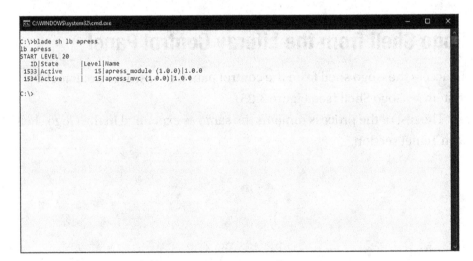

Figure 3-26. *Output of the blade sh lb apress command*

Summary

Liferay DXP portlets enable you to utilize all the features defined in the portlet specifications. The cherries on top are the additional features Liferay provides to maximize the utilization of the framework. Obviously, because the additional Liferay features are Liferay specific, not generic, these portlets cannot be used on any other portlet containers. It does not mean that these additional features do not follow the portlet standards; Liferay has added features such as APIs to improve development with less effort. You learned about these additional portlet modes in this chapter. Another example is the MVC Portlet implementing standard called MVC Pattern, which simplifies portlet development. Generic portlets are also easily deployable on the Liferay DXP portal.

In the next chapter, you learn about a few advanced Liferay concepts.

CHAPTER 4

Advanced Liferay Concepts

This chapter focuses on a few of the essential and advanced concepts of Liferay DXP. You learn how to set communication between two portlets using inter-portlet communication. There are several approaches to IPC, including IPC via *events*, an approach that is commonly used in the industry because of its versatility. Another critical concept—the *message bus*—is also covered in this chapter so that you understand how messaging works in Liferay for background processes. The most implemented form of the message bus is the asynchronous message bus, mainly used for sending bulk mail or batch-processing tasks. Other important topics covered in this chapter include scheduler implementation and scheduled tasks managed by them, such as periodic reports, and so on.

Inter-Portlet Communication

Inter-portlet communication, or IPC, enables communication between two portlets when are deployed on the same instance of the Liferay DXP server. These portlets can be on the same page or different pages, and there are different approaches to IPC depending on the scenario. This communication entails passing a message and some data from Portlet A to Portlet B. The complete concept of inter-portlet communication is based

© Apoorva Prakash and Shaik Inthiyaz Basha 2022
A. Prakash and S. I. Basha, *Hands- On Liferay DXP*,
https://doi.org/10.1007/978-1-4842-8563-3_4

on two kinds of portlets—a sender and a receiver portlet. They are normal portlets but include extra definitions in their metadata to identify their behavior. The portlet invoking the IPC process is referred to as the sender portlet, whereas the one receiving communication is referred to as the receiver portlet. Sender and receiver portlets are also often referred to as producer portlets and consumer portlets, respectively.

The first Portlet Specification (1.0, JSR 168) had minimal capability for IPC. The only way to achieve IPC was portlet session-based; essentially, just setting attributes in a session's portlet makes data accessible to the other portlets. Then came the Portlet Specification 2.0 (JSR 286). It revolutionized the IPC process. It came up with many improved approaches to achieve IPC, such as events, and so on.

Note   Liferay portals support all types of inter-portlet communication (IPC) enlisted in Portlet Specification 1.0 (JSR 168) and Portlet Specification 2.0 (JSR 286).

There are five ways of achieving IPC; let's review them individually.

IPC via Public Render Parameters

Public Render Parameters (PRPs) are one of the most straightforward mechanisms to achieve inter-portlet communication. These portlets may be on different pages or the same page. This approach to inter-portlet communication works on the render parameters, which multiple portlets can access. This approach works on portlets added to the same page by default Liferay configurations; however, this behavior can be modified using scopes.

To use PRPs, you need to define specific portlet parameters. This portlet acts as the producer portlet. This specified parameter goes to another portlet, which has a specific value. As the producer portlet's parameter is accessible by another portlet, the data being carried by this parameter becomes accessible to another portlet. The portlet accessing the parameter to access data is the consumer portlet in this scenario. To make a portlet a consumer, you specify it in the portlet config, similar to how you defined the producer portlet.

Let's look at this more closely with an example. Consider these two portlets to achieve inter-portlet communication, as shown in Figure 4-1.

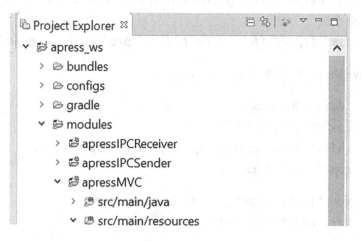

Figure 4-1. *Two portlets to achieve inter-portlet communication*

Select apressIPCSender and apressIPCReceiver; you will work with these portlets to achieve all varieties of IPC. (I do not discuss portlet creation in detail here, as it's covered in Chapter 3.)

In the apressIPCSender portlet, use the code shown in Listing 4-1 to achieve the IPC via the PRP.

Listing 4-1. View.jsp of apressIPCSender Portlet for PRP

```
<%@ taglib uri="http://java.sun.com/jsp/jstl/core"
prefix="c" %>

<%@ taglib uri="http://java.sun.com/portlet_2_0"
prefix="portlet" %>

<%@ taglib uri="http://liferay.com/tld/aui" prefix="aui"
%><%@ taglib uri="http://liferay.com/tld/portlet"
prefix="liferay-portlet" %><%@
taglib uri="http://liferay.com/tld/theme" prefix="liferay-
theme" %><%@
taglib uri="http://liferay.com/tld/ui" prefix="liferay-ui" %>

<liferay-theme:defineObjects />

<portlet:defineObjects />
<div style="padding: 15px">
        <h3><liferay-ui:message key="apressipcsender.
        caption"/></h3>

        <portlet:actionURL name="passMessage"
        var="passMessageURL" />

        <aui:form name="ipcForm" action="${passMessageURL}"
        method="post">
                <aui:input name="inputMessage" type="text"
                label=" Pass Message as Parameter">
            </aui:input>
                <aui:button type="submit"></aui:button>
        </aui:form>
</div>
```

In the code shown in Listing 4-2, you can see the highlighted property, which is crucial to performing the PRP IPC. This property should be the same in the sender and receiver portlets.

Listing 4-2. ApressIPCSenderPortlet Controller Class for PRP

```
package com.apress.handsonliferay.ipc.sender.portlet;

import com.apress.handsonliferay.ipc.sender.constants.
ApressIPCSenderPortletKeys;

import com.liferay.portal.kernel.portlet.bridges.mvc.MVCPortlet;
import com.liferay.portal.kernel.util.ParamUtil;

import java.io.IOException;

import javax.portlet.ActionRequest;
import javax.portlet.ActionResponse;
import javax.portlet.Portlet;
import javax.portlet.PortletException;
import javax.portlet.PortletSession;
import javax.portlet.ProcessAction;
import javax.portlet.RenderRequest;
import javax.portlet.RenderResponse;
import javax.xml.namespace.QName;
import org.osgi.service.component.annotations.Component;

/**
 * @author Apoorva_Inthiyaz
 */
@Component(
        immediate = true,
        property = {
                "com.liferay.portlet.display-
                category=category.ipc",
```

```
            "com.liferay.portlet.header-portlet-css=/css/
            main.css",
            "com.liferay.portlet.instanceable=true",
            "com.liferay.portlet.private-session-
            attributes=false",
            "javax.portlet.display-name=ApressIPCSender",
            "javax.portlet.init-param.template-path=/",
            "javax.portlet.init-param.view-template=/
            view.jsp",
            "javax.portlet.name=" + ApressIPCSenderPortlet
            Keys.APRESSIPCSENDER,
            "javax.portlet.resource-bundle=content.Language",
            "javax.portlet.security-role-ref=power-user,user",
            "javax.portlet.supported-public-render-
            parameter=inputMessage"
            },
        service = Portlet.class
)
public class ApressIPCSenderPortlet extends MVCPortlet {

        public void passMessage(ActionRequest actionRequest,
        ActionResponse actionResponse)
                        throws IOException, PortletException {
                // TODO Auto-generated method stub
                String passMessageVal = ParamUtil.getString
                (actionRequest, "inputMessage","");
                actionResponse.getRenderParameters().
                setValue("inputMessage", passMessageVal);
        }
}
```

In the apressIPCReceiver portlet, use the code shown in Listings 4-3 and 4-4 to achieve IPC via the PRP.

Listing 4-3. View.jsp of the apressIPCReceiver Portlet for PRP

```
<%@ include file="/init.jsp" %>
<h5><liferay-ui:message key="apressipcreceiver.caption"/></h5>

    <h2>Received Message from Public Render Parameter
    :<div style="color:blue">  ${recievedMessage}</div></h2>
```

Listing 4-4. The ApressIPCReceiverPortlet Controller Class for PRP

```
package com.apress.handsonliferay.ipc.receiver.portlet;
import com.apress.handsonliferay.ipc.receiver.constants.
ApressIPCReceiverPortletKeys;
import com.liferay.portal.kernel.portlet.bridges.mvc.MVCPortlet;
import com.liferay.portal.kernel.util.ParamUtil;

import java.io.IOException;

import javax.portlet.Event;
import javax.portlet.EventRequest;
import javax.portlet.EventResponse;
import javax.portlet.Portlet;
import javax.portlet.PortletException;
import javax.portlet.PortletSession;
import javax.portlet.ProcessEvent;
import javax.portlet.RenderRequest;
import javax.portlet.RenderResponse;

import org.osgi.service.component.annotations.Component;

/**
 * @author Apoorva_Inthiyaz
 */
@Component(
        immediate = true,
```

```
        property = {
                "com.liferay.portlet.display-
                category=category.ipc",
                "com.liferay.portlet.header-portlet-css=/css/
                main.css",
                "com.liferay.portlet.instanceable=true",
                "com.liferay.portlet.private-session-
                attributes=false",
                "javax.portlet.display-name=ApressIPCReceiver",
                "javax.portlet.init-param.template-path=/",
                "javax.portlet.init-param.view-template=/
                view.jsp",
                "javax.portlet.name=" + ApressIPCReceiverPortlet
                Keys.APRESSIPCRECEIVER,
                "javax.portlet.resource-bundle=content.Language",
"javax.portlet.security-role-ref=power-user,user",
                "javax.portlet.supported-public-render-
                parameter=inputMessage",
                "javax.portlet.supported-processing-
                event=produceMessage;http://inthiyaz.com"
        },
        service = Portlet.class
)
public class ApressIPCReceiverPortlet extends MVCPortlet {
        @Override
        public void doView(RenderRequest renderRequest,
        RenderResponse renderResponse)
                        throws IOException, PortletException {
                // TODO Auto-generated method stub
                String passMessageVal = ParamUtil.getString
                (renderRequest, "inputMessage","");
```

```
System.out.println("Received Message
"+passMessageVal);
renderRequest.setAttribute("recievedMessage",
passMessageVal);

PortletSession portletSession = renderRequest.
getPortletSession();
renderRequest.setAttribute("recievedSession
Message",

                (String)portletSession.
                getAttribute("Liferay_Shared_
                Session_Para",PortletSession.
                APPLICATION_SCOPE));
super.doView(renderRequest, renderResponse);
}
}
```

As you can see, `javax.portlet.supported-public-render-parameter=inputMessage` should be the same in the sender and receiver portlets' container component property to achieve IPC via the Public Render Parameter.

Once you deploy both portlets to your Liferay server, you can add both portlets to your Liferay page, as shown in Figures 4-2 and 4-3. If you add two portlets side by side, it will be more helpful to see the output.

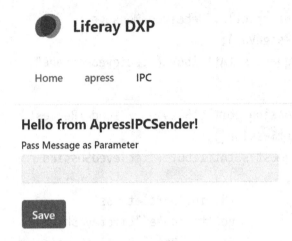

Liferay DXP

Home   apress   IPC

Hello from ApressIPCSender!

Pass Message as Parameter

Save

Figure 4-2. *Output screen of the ApressIPCSender portlet for PRP*

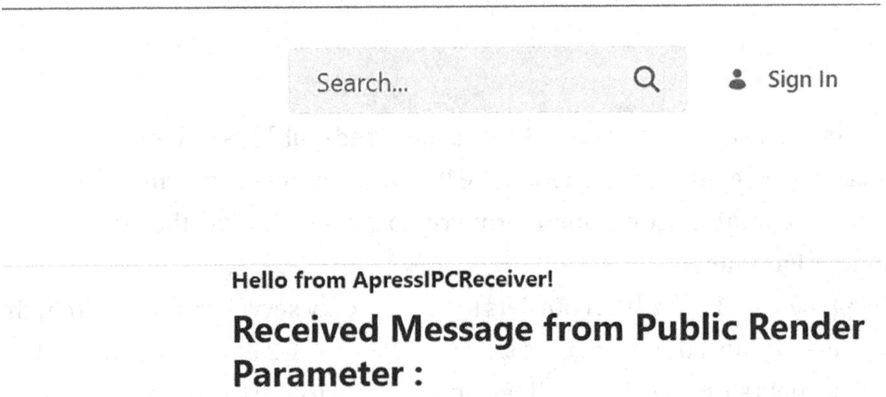

Search...   🔍   👤 Sign In

Hello from ApressIPCReceiver!

Received Message from Public Render Parameter :

Figure 4-3. *Output screen of the ApressIPCReceiver portlet for PRP*

When you submit text from the apressIPCSender portlet, that text will be received by the apressIPCReceiver portlet.

IPC via Private Session Attributes

This approach to inter-portlet communication is very similar to the previous approach. The only difference is that instead of specifying a public parameter, the complete portlet session is accessible to other portlets. The producer and consumer portlets can be available on the same page or another page.

Let's look at this with an example that uses the same apressIPCSender and apressIPCReceiver portlets to achieve a Private Session Attributes (PSA) IPC.

In the apressIPCSender portlet controller, use the code shown in Listing 4-5 to achieve IPC via Private Session Attributes. You can see the highlighted property, which is vital to performing Private Session Attributes IPC, and this property should be the same in the sender and receivers portlets.

Listing 4-5. ApressIPCSenderPortlet Controller Class for PSA

```
package com.apress.handsonliferay.ipc.sender.portlet;

import com.apress.handsonliferay.ipc.sender.constants.
ApressIPCSenderPortletKeys;

import com.liferay.portal.kernel.portlet.bridges.mvc.MVCPortlet;
import com.liferay.portal.kernel.util.ParamUtil;

import java.io.IOException;

import javax.portlet.ActionRequest;
import javax.portlet.ActionResponse;
import javax.portlet.Portlet;
import javax.portlet.PortletException;
import javax.portlet.PortletSession;
import javax.portlet.ProcessAction;
```

```java
import javax.portlet.RenderRequest;
import javax.portlet.RenderResponse;
import javax.xml.namespace.QName;

import org.osgi.service.component.annotations.Component;

/**
 * @author Inthiyaz
 */
@Component(
        immediate = true,
        property = {
                "com.liferay.portlet.display-
                category=category.ipc",
                "com.liferay.portlet.header-portlet-css=/css/
                main.css",
                "com.liferay.portlet.instanceable=true",
                "com.liferay.portlet.private-session-
                attributes=false",
                "javax.portlet.display-name=ApressIPCSender",
                "javax.portlet.init-param.template-path=/",
                "javax.portlet.init-param.view-template=/
                view.jsp",
                "javax.portlet.name=" + ApressIPCSenderPortlet
                Keys.APRESSIPCSENDER,
                "javax.portlet.resource-bundle=content.Language",
                "javax.portlet.security-role-ref=power-user,user",
                "javax.portlet.supported-public-render-
                parameter=inputMessage",
                "javax.portlet.supported-publishing-
                event=produceMessage;http://inthiyaz.com"
        },
```

```java
    service = Portlet.class
)
public class ApressIPCSenderPortlet extends MVCPortlet {

    public void passMessage(ActionRequest actionRequest,
    ActionResponse actionResponse)
                        throws IOException, PortletException {
        // TODO Auto-generated method stub
        String passMessageVal = ParamUtil.getString
        (actionRequest, "inputMessage","");
        actionResponse.getRenderParameters().
        setValue("inputMessage", passMessageVal);
    }

    @Override
    public void doView(RenderRequest renderRequest,
    RenderResponse renderResponse)
                        throws IOException, PortletException {
        // TODO Auto-generated method stub
        PortletSession portletSession = renderRequest.
        getPortletSession();
        portletSession.setAttribute("Liferay_
        Shared_Session_Para", "Session Param",
        PortletSession.APPLICATION_SCOPE);
        super.doView(renderRequest, renderResponse);
    }
}
```

In the apressIPCReceiver portlet, use the code shown in Listings 4-6 and 4-7 to achieve IPC via Private Session Attributes. Observe that com.liferay.portlet.private-session-attributes=false should be identical in the sender and receiver portlets container's component property to achieve IPC via Private Session Attributes.

Listing 4-6. View.jsp of apressIPCReceiver Portlet for PSA

```
<%@ include file="/init.jsp" %>

        <h5><liferay-ui:message key="apressipcreceiver.
        caption"/></h5>

        <h2>Received Message from Public Render Parameter
        :<div style="color:blue">  ${recievedMessage}</div></h2>

        <h2>Received Message from Session Parameter :<div
        style="color:red">  ${recievedSessionMessage}</div></h2>
```

Listing 4-7. ApressIPCReceiverPortlet Controller Class for PSA

```
package com.apress.handsonliferay.ipc.receiver.portlet;

import com.apress.handsonliferay.ipc.receiver.constants.
ApressIPCReceiverPortletKeys;
import com.liferay.portal.kernel.portlet.bridges.mvc.MVCPortlet;
import com.liferay.portal.kernel.util.ParamUtil;

import java.io.IOException;

import javax.portlet.Event;
import javax.portlet.EventRequest;
import javax.portlet.EventResponse;
import javax.portlet.Portlet;
import javax.portlet.PortletException;
import javax.portlet.PortletSession;
import javax.portlet.ProcessEvent;
import javax.portlet.RenderRequest;
import javax.portlet.RenderResponse;

import org.osgi.service.component.annotations.Component;
```

```java
/**
 * @author Inthiyaz
 */
@Component(
        immediate = true,
        property = {
                "com.liferay.portlet.display-
                category=category.ipc",
                "com.liferay.portlet.header-portlet-css=/css/
                main.css",
                "com.liferay.portlet.instanceable=true",
                "com.liferay.portlet.private-session-
                attributes=false",
                "javax.portlet.display-name=ApressIPCReceiver",
                "javax.portlet.init-param.template-path=/",
                "javax.portlet.init-param.view-template=/
                view.jsp",
                "javax.portlet.name=" + ApressIPCReceiverPortlet
                Keys.APRESSIPCRECEIVER,
                "javax.portlet.resource-bundle=content.Language",
                "javax.portlet.security-role-ref=power-user,user",
                "javax.portlet.supported-public-render-
                parameter=inputMessage",
                "javax.portlet.supported-processing-
                event=produceMessage;http://inthiyaz.com"
        },
        service = Portlet.class
)
public class ApressIPCReceiverPortlet extends MVCPortlet {
        @Override
        public void doView(RenderRequest renderRequest,
        RenderResponse renderResponse)
```

```
                    throws IOException, PortletException {
// TODO Auto-generated method stub
String passMessageVal = ParamUtil.getString
(renderRequest, "inputMessage","");
System.out.println("Received Message
"+passMessageVal);
renderRequest.setAttribute("recievedMessage",
passMessageVal);

PortletSession portletSession = renderRequest.
getPortletSession();
renderRequest.setAttribute("recievedSession
Message",
                    (String)portletSession.
                    getAttribute("Liferay_Shared_
                    Session_Para",PortletSession.
                    APPLICATION_SCOPE));
super.doView(renderRequest, renderResponse);
                    }
}
```

After you deploy these portlets in your Liferay server, you will see the output shown in Figure 4-4.

Figure 4-4. *Output screens of ApressIPCSender and ApressIPCReceiver portlets for PSA*

IPC via Server-Side Events

Events-based IPC was introduced in Portlet Specification 2.0 (JSR 286). This new approach was implemented using server-side events. According to this mechanism, the producer portlet produces a possibility that other consumer portlets can consume. Figure 4-5 shows the working flow of IPC via server-side events.

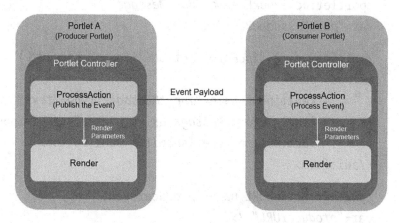

Figure 4-5. *Working flow of IPC via server-side events*

By default, this mode also works on portlets added to the same page. But using the following property in `portal-ext.properties`, you can access the portal.

`portlet.event.distribution=layout-set`

Let's illustrate this concept with an example. In the `apressIPCSender` portlet, use the code shown in Listings 4-8 and 4-9 to achieve IPC via server-side events.

Listing 4-8. View.jsp of the apressIPCSender Portlet for an Event

```
<%@ include file="/init.jsp" %>

<div style="padding: 15px">
        <h3><liferay-ui:message key="apressipcsender.
        caption"/></h3>

        <portlet:actionURL name="passMessage"
        var="passMessageURL" />

        <aui:form name="ipcForm" action="${passMessageURL}"
        method="post">
                <aui:input name="inputMessage" type="text"
                label=" Pass Message as Parameter"></aui:input>
                <aui:button type="submit"></aui:button>
        </aui:form>

        <portlet:actionURL name="producerevent"
        var="producerURL" />

        <aui:form name="ipceventForm" action="${producerURL}"
        method="post">
                <aui:input name="eventmessage" type="text"
                label=" Pass Message for Event"></aui:input>
                <aui:button type="submit"></aui:button>
        </aui:form>
</div>
```

Listing 4-9. ApressIPCSenderPortlet Controller Class for an Event

```
package com.apress.handsonliferay.ipc.sender.portlet;

import com.apress.handsonliferay.ipc.sender.constants.
ApressIPCSenderPortletKeys;
```

```java
import com.liferay.portal.kernel.portlet.bridges.mvc.MVCPortlet;
import com.liferay.portal.kernel.util.ParamUtil;

import java.io.IOException;

import javax.portlet.ActionRequest;
import javax.portlet.ActionResponse;
import javax.portlet.Portlet;
import javax.portlet.PortletException;
import javax.portlet.PortletSession;
import javax.portlet.ProcessAction;
import javax.portlet.RenderRequest;
import javax.portlet.RenderResponse;
import javax.xml.namespace.QName;

import org.osgi.service.component.annotations.Component;
/**
 * @author Inthiyaz
 */
@Component(
        immediate = true,
        property = {
                "com.liferay.portlet.display-
                category=category.ipc",
                "com.liferay.portlet.header-portlet-css=/css/
                main.css",
                "com.liferay.portlet.instanceable=true",
                "com.liferay.portlet.private-session-
                attributes=false",
                "javax.portlet.display-name=ApressIPCSender",
                "javax.portlet.init-param.template-path=/",
                "javax.portlet.init-param.view-template=/
                view.jsp",
```

```
                    "javax.portlet.name=" + ApressIPCSenderPortlet
                    Keys.APRESSIPCSENDER,
                    "javax.portlet.resource-bundle=content.Language",
                    "javax.portlet.security-role-ref=power-user,user",
                    "javax.portlet.supported-public-render-
                    parameter=inputMessage",
                    "javax.portlet.supported-publishing-
                    event=produceMessage;http://inthiyaz.com"
        },
        service = Portlet.class
)
public class ApressIPCSenderPortlet extends MVCPortlet {

        public void passMessage(ActionRequest actionRequest,
        ActionResponse actionResponse)
                        throws IOException, PortletException {
                // TODO Auto-generated method stub
                String passMessageVal = ParamUtil.getString
                (actionRequest, "inputMessage","");
                actionResponse.getRenderParameters().
                setValue("inputMessage", passMessageVal);
        }

        @Override
        public void doView(RenderRequest renderRequest,
        RenderResponse renderResponse)
                        throws IOException, PortletException {
                // TODO Auto-generated method stub
                PortletSession portletSession = renderRequest.
                getPortletSession();
                portletSession.setAttribute("Liferay_
                Shared_Session_Para", "Session Param",
                PortletSession.APPLICATION_SCOPE);
```

```
        super.doView(renderRequest, renderResponse);
    }

    @ProcessAction(name = "producerevent")
    public void producerEvent(ActionRequest
    actionRequest,ActionResponse actionResponse) {
            String message = ParamUtil.getString
            (actionRequest, "eventmessage","");
            QName qName = new QName("http://inthiyaz.
            com","produceMessage");
            System.out.println("----"+message);
            actionResponse.setEvent(qName, message);
    }

}
```

In the apressIPCReceiver portlet, use the code shown in Listings 4-10 and 4-11 to achieve IPC via server-side events.

Listing 4-10. View.jsp of the apressIPCReceiver Portlet for an Event

```
<%@ include file="/init.jsp" %>
        <h5><liferay-ui:message key="apressipcreceiver.
        caption"/></h5>

        <h2>Received Message from Public Render Parameter
        :<div style="color:blue">  ${recievedMessage}</div></h2>

        <h2>Received Message from Session Parameter :<div
        style="color:red">  ${recievedSessionMessage}</
        div></h2>

        <h2>Received Message from Event Parameter : <div
        style="color:green"> ${message} </div></h2>
```

Listing 4-11. ApressIPCReceiverPortlet Controller Class for
an Event

```
package com.apress.handsonliferay.ipc.receiver.portlet;

import com.apress.handsonliferay.ipc.receiver.constants.
ApressIPCReceiverPortletKeys;
import com.liferay.portal.kernel.portlet.bridges.mvc.MVCPortlet;
import com.liferay.portal.kernel.util.ParamUtil;

import java.io.IOException;

import javax.portlet.Event;
import javax.portlet.EventRequest;
import javax.portlet.EventResponse;
import javax.portlet.Portlet;
import javax.portlet.PortletException;
import javax.portlet.PortletSession;
import javax.portlet.ProcessEvent;
import javax.portlet.RenderRequest;
import javax.portlet.RenderResponse;

import org.osgi.service.component.annotations.Component;

/**
 * @author Inthiyaz
 */
@Component(
        immediate = true,
        property = {
                "com.liferay.portlet.display-
                category=category.ipc",
                "com.liferay.portlet.header-portlet-css=/css/
                main.css",
```

```
            "com.liferay.portlet.instanceable=true",
            "com.liferay.portlet.private-session-
            attributes=false",
            "javax.portlet.display-name=ApressIPCReceiver",
            "javax.portlet.init-param.template-path=/",
            "javax.portlet.init-param.view-template=/
            view.jsp",
            "javax.portlet.name=" +
            ApressIPCReceiverPortletKeys.APRESSIPCRECEIVER,
            "javax.portlet.resource-bundle=content.Language",
            "javax.portlet.security-role-ref=power-user,user",
            "javax.portlet.supported-public-render-
            parameter=inputMessage",
            "javax.portlet.supported-processing-
            event=produceMessage;http://inthiyaz.com"
        },
        service = Portlet.class
)
public class ApressIPCReceiverPortlet extends MVCPortlet {
        @Override
        public void doView(RenderRequest renderRequest,
        RenderResponse renderResponse)
                        throws IOException, PortletException {
                // TODO Auto-generated method stub
                String passMessageVal = ParamUtil.getString
                (renderRequest, "inputMessage","");
                System.out.println("Received Message
                "+passMessageVal);
                renderRequest.setAttribute("recievedMessage",
                passMessageVal);
```

```
            PortletSession portletSession = renderRequest.
            getPortletSession();
            renderRequest.setAttribute("recievedSessio
            nMessage",
                            (String)portletSession.
                            getAttribute("Liferay_Shared_
                            Session_Para",PortletSession.
                            APPLICATION_SCOPE));
            super.doView(renderRequest, renderResponse);
            }

    @ProcessEvent(qname = "{http://inthiyaz.com}
    produceMessage")
            public void consumeMessage(EventRequest
            eventRequest,EventResponse eventResponse) {
            Event event = eventRequest.getEvent();
            String receivedValue = (String)event.getValue();
            eventRequest.setAttribute("message",
            receivedValue);
            System.out.println("Event Message "+
            receivedValue);

    }
}
```

You can observe that javax.portlet.supported-publishing-event=produceMessage;http://inthiyaz.com should be identical in the sender and receiver portlets container's component property to achieve IPC via Private Session Attributes.

When you deploy both portlets in your Liferay server, you will see the output shown in Figure 4-6.

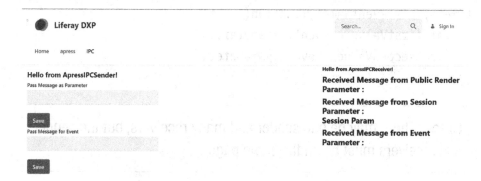

Figure 4-6. *Output screens of ApressIPCSender and ApressIPCReceiver Portlets for an event*

Client-Side IPC via Ajax

Client-Side inter-portlet communication is one of the approaches wherein IPC is achieved from the client side instead of the server side. This is one of two approaches to achieve this. Client-side IPC can communicate with a portlet on the same page. Because client-side IPC uses JavaScript to communicate, all portlets that participate in IPC must be on the same page. Liferay provides a JavaScript library for its implementation. The client-side IPC using Ajax is very similar to event-based IPC; the difference is that this is achieved by Ajax instead of by a server-side event.

Let's look at this with an example. In the apressIPCSender portlet, use the following code to achieve IPC via client-side Ajax.

```
Liferay.fire('eventName',{
        parameter1: value1,
        parameter2: value2
});
```

In the apressIPCReceiver portlet, use the following code to achieve IPC via client-side Ajax.

```
Liferay.on('eventName',function(event) {
    var firstValue = event.parameter1,
    var  secondValue = event.parameter2
});
```

Note   There may be one sender and many receivers, but the sender and receivers must be on the same page.

Client-Side IPC via Cookies

Like client-side IPC with Ajax, you can achieve IPC through browser cookies. The data is stored in cookies, and other portlets will access this information. However, this comes with limitations regarding data privacy, which is why this is rarely used. Another shortcoming is that if cookie access is disabled on the browser, this will fail. There are several ways to achieve this, as you can set and read cookies using plain JavaScript or jQuery. The following sample code in JavaScript illustrates this approach.

Setting the cookie:

```
function setIPCCookie() {
    document.cookie = "bookName=Hands On Liferay DXP";
}
```

Reading the cookie:

```
function getIPCCookie() {
  var cookies = "; " + document.cookie;
  var keyValues = cookies.split(";bookName=");
  if (keyValues.length == 2)
    return keyValues.pop().split(";").shift();
  else
    return '';
}
```

This explains how IPC can be achieved with different approaches; in the next section, you learn about the Liferay message bus.

Liferay Message Bus

Liferay's message bus is a loosely coupled approach to exchanging messages. This loose coupling lets message producers continue to the next task/instruction while the consumer gets the message and starts processing it. Inherently, this is a service-level API that components can use to send and receive messages. This Message Bus API is part of Liferay's global class loader, making it accessible across the Liferay server. This works well in a clustered environment.

The message bus is very helpful in scenarios where you must do parallel processing. For example, you need to update the search index once the data is updated, but user flow need not stop for it. You can pass messages to a message bus with essential data to update the search index, while the user flow can return with the data update process.

The message bus system contains the following components:

> **Message bus**: The message bus ensures the transfer of messages between senders and listeners. The following code is used to create a message bus.
>
> com.liferay.portal.kernel.messaging.MessageBus.
> .sendMessage(destinationName, messageobj)
>
> **Destination**: A destination is an address to which listeners are registered to receive messages. Message bus destinations are based on the destination configurations and registered as OSGI services, and they detect the destination services and manage their associated destinations. There are three types of destinations:

- Parallel destination

- Serial destination

- Synchronous destination

Destinations are based on the
DestinationConfiguration (com.liferay.portal.
kernel.messaging.DestinationConfiguration),
which provides three static methods for creating
various types of destinations:

- createParallelDestinationConfiguration(String
  destinationName)

- createSerialDestinationConfiguration(String
  destinationName)

- createSynchronousDestinationConfiguration
  (String destinationName)

Listener: A listener is the receiver of the messages.
It consumes messages received at destinations and
processes them. In Liferay, you have three ways for
message listeners to listen to messages:

- Automatic Registration as a Component (see
  Listing 4-12)

Listing 4-12. MessageBusRegisteredSynchronous
MessageListener Class

```
package com.handsonliferay.messagebus.event.listener;

import com.liferay.portal.kernel.log.Log;
import com.liferay.portal.kernel.log.LogFactoryUtil;
import com.liferay.portal.kernel.messaging.Message;
import com.liferay.portal.kernel.messaging.MessageListener;
```

```java
public class MessageBusRegisteredSynchronousMessageListener
implements MessageListener {
        @Override
        public void receive(Message message) {
    //Do your job here
                try {
                        _log.info("Message::"+message);

                }
                catch (Exception e) {
                        e.printStackTrace();
                }

        }

        private static final Log _log = LogFactoryUtil.getLog
                (MessageBusRegisteredSynchronousMessageListener.
                class);

}
```

- Registering via a message bus reference (see Listing 4-13)

Listing 4-13. MessageBusRegistrator Class

```java
package com.handsonliferay.messagebus.register;

import com.handsonliferay.messagebus.event.listener.
MessageBusRegisteredParallelMessageListener;
import com.handsonliferay.messagebus.event.listener.
MessageBusRegisteredSerialMessageListener;
import com.handsonliferay.messagebus.event.listener.
MessageBusRegisteredSynchronousMessageListener;
import com.liferay.portal.kernel.log.Log;
```

```java
import com.liferay.portal.kernel.log.LogFactoryUtil;
import com.liferay.portal.kernel.messaging.MessageBus;
import com.liferay.portal.kernel.messaging.MessageListener;
import com.handsonliferay.messagebus.constants.
LiferayMessageBusPortletKeys;

import org.osgi.service.component.annotations.Activate;
import org.osgi.service.component.annotations.Component;
import org.osgi.service.component.annotations.Deactivate;
import org.osgi.service.component.annotations.Reference;

@Component (
          immediate = true,
          service = MessageBusRegistrator.class
      )
public class MessageBusRegistrator{
    @Reference
    private MessageBus _messageBus;
    private MessageListener _messageListenerParallel;
    private MessageListener _messageListenerSerail;
    private MessageListener _messageListenerSynchronius;
        private static final Log _log = LogFactoryUtil.getLog
        (MessageBusRegistrator.class);

        @Activate
    protected void activate() {
            _messageListenerParallel = new
            MessageBusRegisteredParallelMessageListener();
        _messageBus.registerMessageListener(Liferay
        MessageBusPortletKeys.DESTINATION_PARALLEL, _
        messageListenerParallel);
        _log.info("Message Listener Registered.."+_
        messageListenerParallel);
```

```
_messageListenerSerail = new
MessageBusRegisteredSerialMessageListener();
_messageBus.registerMessageListener(LiferayMessageBus
PortletKeys.DESTINATION_SERIAL, _messageListenerSerail);
_log.info("Message Listener Registered.."+_
messageListenerSerail);

_messageListenerSynchronius = new
MessageBusRegisteredSynchronousMessageListener();
_messageBus.registerMessageListener(Liferay
MessageBusPortletKeys.DESTINATION_SYNCHRONOUS, _
messageListenerSynchronius);
_log.info("Message Listener Registered.."+_
messageListenerSynchronius);
}

@Deactivate
protected void deactivate() {
    _messageBus.unregisterMessageListener
    (LiferayMessageBusPortletKeys.DESTINATION_PARALLEL, _
    messageListenerParallel);
    _log.info("Message Listener Unregistered.."+_
    messageListenerParallel);

    _messageBus.unregisterMessageListener
    (LiferayMessageBusPortletKeys.DESTINATION_SERIAL, _
    messageListenerSerail);
    _log.info("Message Listener Unregistered.."+_
    messageListenerSerail);

    _messageBus.unregisterMessageListener
    (LiferayMessageBusPortletKeys.DESTINATION_
    SYNCHRONOUS, _messageListenerSynchronius);
```

```
        _log.info("Message Listener Unregistered.."+_
        messageListenerSynchronius);
    }
}
```

- Registering directly to the destination (see Listing 4-14)

Listing 4-14. DestinationListenerRegistrator Class

```
package com.handsonliferay.messagebus.register;

import com.handsonliferay.messagebus.event.listener.
DestinationRegisteredParallelMessageListener;
import com.liferay.portal.kernel.log.Log;
import com.liferay.portal.kernel.log.LogFactoryUtil;
import com.liferay.portal.kernel.messaging.Destination;
import com.liferay.portal.kernel.messaging.MessageListener;
import org.osgi.service.component.annotations.Activate;
import org.osgi.service.component.annotations.Component;
import org.osgi.service.component.annotations.Deactivate;
import org.osgi.service.component.annotations.Reference;

@Component (
            immediate = true,
            service = DestinationListenerRegistrator.class
        )
public class DestinationListenerRegistrator{

    private MessageListener _messageListener;
        private static final Log _log = LogFactoryUtil.getLog
        (DestinationListenerRegistrator.class);
```

```
@Reference(target = "(destination.name="+"Destination
message"+")")
private Destination _destinationParellel;

    @Activate
protected void activate() {
            _messageListener = new
            DestinationRegisteredParallelMessageListener();
            _destinationParellel.register(_
            messageListener);
    _log.info("Message Listener Registered.."+_
    messageListener);
}
@Deactivate
protected void deactivate() {
    _destinationParellel.unregister(_messageListener);
    _log.info("Message Listener Unregistered.."+_
    messageListener);
}}
```

> **Sender**: A sender is the one who sends messages to
> start the processing in the listener. This is the one who
> initiates the process.

You can see this whole process with the help of Figure 4-7. As the name suggests, you can send messages directly using the message bus. Use the same MessageSenderServiceImpl class for the two types of message busses as well (see Listings 4-15 and 4-16).

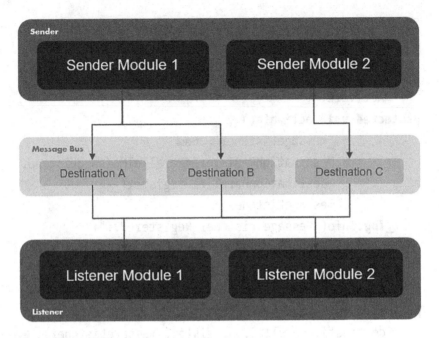

Figure 4-7. *Message bus*

Synchronous Message Bus

As the name suggests, the sender will sync with the listener until the message processing is complete. Here, the sender waits until it gets a response from the listener. The example code in Listing 4-16 helps illustrate this concept.

Listing 4-15. MessageSenderServiceImpl Class for a Synchronous Message

```
package com.handsonliferay.messagebus.service;

import com.liferay.portal.kernel.log.Log;
import com.liferay.portal.kernel.log.LogFactoryUtil;
import com.liferay.portal.kernel.messaging.Destination;
```

```java
import com.liferay.portal.kernel.messaging.
DestinationStatistics;
import com.liferay.portal.kernel.messaging.Message;
import com.liferay.portal.kernel.messaging.MessageBus;
import com.liferay.portal.kernel.messaging.MessageBusException;
import com.liferay.portal.kernel.messaging.MessageBusUtil;
import com.liferay.portal.kernel.messaging.MessageListener;

import java.util.ArrayList;
import java.util.List;
import java.util.Set;

import org.osgi.service.component.annotations.Component;
import org.osgi.service.component.annotations.Reference;

@Component(
          immediate = true,
          service = MessageSenderServiceImpl.class
       )
public class MessageSenderServiceImpl{
       @Reference
    private MessageBus _messageBus;
       private static final Log _log = LogFactoryUtil.getLog
       (MessageSenderServiceImpl.class);
       public void sendMessageToDestination(String
       message,String destinationName) {

       Message messageobj = new Message();
       messageobj.put("message", message);
       _messageBus.sendMessage(destinationName, messageobj);
    }

              public void sendSynchronousMessageToDestination
              (String message,String destinationName) {
```

```
Message messageobj = new Message();
messageobj.put("message", message);
try {
                MessageBusUtil.sendSynchronousMessage
                (destinationName, messageobj);
                //MessageBusUtil.sendSynchronousMessage
                (destinationName, message, timeout)
        } catch (MessageBusException e) {
                // TODO Auto-generated catch block
                e.printStackTrace();
        }
    }

}
```

Asynchronous Message Bus

Here, the sender and listener are not in sync. The sender can continue processing without waiting for a response from the listener, referred to as *send and forget asynchronous message bus*. It is possible to receive a notification in the form of a callback, also referred to as a *callback asynchronous message bus*. The sender can also be configured to receive a callback. Listing 4-16 shows an example of this.

Listing 4-16. MessageSenderServiceImpl Class for Synchronous and Asynchronous Messages

```
package com.handsonliferay.messagebus.service;

import com.liferay.portal.kernel.log.Log;
import com.liferay.portal.kernel.log.LogFactoryUtil;
import com.liferay.portal.kernel.messaging.Destination;
```

```java
import com.liferay.portal.kernel.messaging.
DestinationStatistics;
import com.liferay.portal.kernel.messaging.Message;
import com.liferay.portal.kernel.messaging.MessageBus;
import com.liferay.portal.kernel.messaging.MessageBusException;
import com.liferay.portal.kernel.messaging.MessageBusUtil;
import com.liferay.portal.kernel.messaging.MessageListener;

import java.util.ArrayList;
import java.util.List;
import java.util.Set;

import org.osgi.service.component.annotations.Component;
import org.osgi.service.component.annotations.Reference;

@Component(
            immediate = true,
            service = MessageSenderServiceImpl.class
        )
public class MessageSenderServiceImpl{
        @Reference
    private MessageBus _messageBus;
        private static final Log _log = LogFactoryUtil.getLog
        (MessageSenderServiceImpl.class);
        public void sendMessageToDestination(String
        message,String destinationName) {

        Message messageobj = new Message();
        messageobj.put("message", message);
        _messageBus.sendMessage(destinationName, messageobj);
    }

        public DestinationStatistics
        getDestinationStatistics(String destinationName) {
```

```
            Destination destination = _messageBus.get
            Destination(destinationName);
            Set<MessageListener> listeners = destination.
            getMessageListeners();
            for (MessageListener curListener : listeners) {
        }
            DestinationStatistics dstatiStrics =
            destination.getDestinationStatistics();
            return dstatiStrics;

    }

    public List<String> getListeners(String
    destinationName) {
            Destination destination = _messageBus.get
            Destination(destinationName);
            Set<MessageListener> listeners = destination.
            getMessageListeners();
            List<String> listenersList = new
            ArrayList<String>();
            for (MessageListener curListener : listeners) {
                    listenersList.add(curListener.
                    toString());
        }
            return listenersList;

    }

    public void sendSynchronousMessageToDestination(String
    message,String destinationName) {

    Message messageobj = new Message();
    messageobj.put("message", message);
    try {
```

```
        MessageBusUtil.sendSynchronousMessage
        (destinationName, messageobj);
        //MessageBusUtil.sendSynchronousMessage
        (destinationName, message, timeout)
    } catch (MessageBusException e) {
        // TODO Auto-generated catch block
        e.printStackTrace();
    }
  }

}
```

This explains how the Liferay message bus can be implemented; in the next section, you learn about the Liferay scheduler.

Liferay Scheduler

Schedulers do a simple job—they run a piece of code at a certain point in time, in a time-set repetition. Confused?? Let's look at this more closely. Schedules are the core of many applications worldwide. They can be used for publishing reports, sending subscription emails, running batch jobs, and similar tasks. These tasks need to run monthly, weekly, and so on. A scheduler automates these tasks. A scheduler is nothing but a function invoked at a certain time instead of by any action, and that's why it is called a scheduler. Liferay DXP provides excellent support for developing schedulers. Figure 4-8 shows the working flow of the Liferay scheduler.

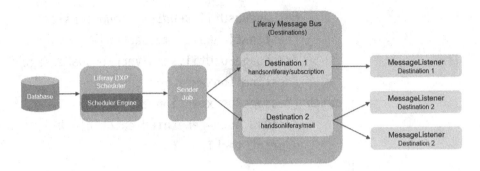

Figure 4-8. *Working flow of the Liferay scheduler*

Liferay's scheduler mechanism was developed on top of the Quartz scheduler engine, which is an open-source Java implementation for scheduling jobs. Liferay's implementation of Quartz makes it simple to use and easy to implement, which you'll see soon.

Before starting the implementation, you should know about the storage types. Liferay DXP provides three storage types:

1. Memory (`StorageType.MEMORY`): This storage type does not persist job information anywhere (only in memory) that is not cluster-aware. So, if there is a server outage at the scheduled time, the scheduler will not run, and in case it is used in a clustered environment, it will run *n* number of times, causing duplicate execution of code, where *n* is the number of nodes in the cluster.

2. Memory Clustered (`StorageType.MEMORY_CLUSTERED`): This storage type is similar to the previous `MEMORY` storage type, where the job information is kept in memory. Still, the only difference is that this type is cluster-aware. This means it will be affected during outages but will not rerun in a clustered environment. This is the default storage type.

3. StorageType.PERSISTED: In contrast to the
    MEMORY storage type, job details are persisted in
    the database. This takes care of the missed job in
    the case of outages and it is cluster-aware. This
    information is stored in the database tables.

In the case of the clustered environment, using either MEMORY_
CLUSTERED or PERSISTED is recommended to ensure your job doesn't run
on every node. The MEMORY type is recommended if the job needs to run
on all the nodes of the cluster (such as taking periodic thread dumps,
and so on).

Let's implement some code to get this running (see Listing 4-17).

Listing 4-17. SchedulerServiceImpl Class for Scheduler

```
package com.handsonliferay.scheduler.service;

import com.liferay.portal.kernel.log.Log;
import com.liferay.portal.kernel.log.LogFactoryUtil;
import com.liferay.portal.kernel.messaging.Message;
import com.liferay.portal.kernel.scheduler.
SchedulerEngineHelper;
import com.liferay.portal.kernel.scheduler.SchedulerException;
import com.liferay.portal.kernel.scheduler.StorageType;
import com.liferay.portal.kernel.scheduler.Trigger;
import com.liferay.portal.kernel.scheduler.TriggerFactory;
import java.util.TimeZone;
import org.osgi.service.component.annotations.Component;
import org.osgi.service.component.annotations.Reference;
```

```java
@Component(
        immediate = true,
        service = SchedulerServiceImpl.class
    )
public class SchedulerServiceImpl{
    public void createSchedule(String jobName, String
    groupName, String cron, String destinationName, String
    description)
                    throws SchedulerException {
        Trigger trigger = _triggerFactory.
        createTrigger(jobName,groupName,null,null,
        cron,TimeZone.getDefault());
        Message message = new Message();
        message.put("data",jobName+":"+groupName);
        _schedulerEngineHelper.schedule(trigger,
        StorageType.PERSISTED, description,
        destinationName, message, exceptionsMaxSize);

    }
    public static int exceptionsMaxSize = 10;

    @Reference
    private SchedulerEngineHelper _schedulerEngineHelper;

    @Reference
    private TriggerFactory _triggerFactory;

    private static final Log _log = LogFactoryUtil.getLog
    (SchedulerServiceImpl.class);
}
```

Summary

This chapter covered a few advanced concepts of Liferay DXP. Inter-portlet communication is practically vital for real-world applications, and in most applications, IPC via events is used because of its versatility. Message busses also play a vital role, and the most commonly implemented form is the asynchronous message bus. It's primarily used for sending bulk mail or batch-processing tasks. The scheduler implementation manages the execution of scheduled tasks, such as periodic reports.

In the next chapter, you will learn about the Liferay Service Builder.

CHAPTER 5

Service Builder Concepts

This chapter focuses on the Service Builder. The Service Builder is the easiest way to create a service and a DAO layer for portlets with the help of a master file. A lot of boilerplate code is generated when services are built using this file. This file helps generate the mappings. In this chapter, you learn everything about this process and the different ways to fetch data from the database.

Introduction to the Service Builder

The Service Builder is one tool that makes Liferay stand out in connecting services to custom portlets in the database. It's easy, accurate, and effective. The Service Builder can generate all necessary objects, classes, and methods for database connectivity with a custom module. In short, you can say that it generates a complete service and a DAO layer. Not only this, but it also generates SQL scripts so that when the portlet is deployed, it will generate the necessary tables in the database. The Service Builder is dependent on a file called service.xml. All magic starts in this file. This file contains all the information needed for service generation. Liferay DXP's Service Builder is slightly different than the older version.

© Apoorva Prakash and Shaik Inthiyaz Basha 2022
A. Prakash and S. I. Basha, *Hands- On Liferay DXP*,
https://doi.org/10.1007/978-1-4842-8563-3_5

Now, it does not generate a `service.jar` file. Instead, it creates two new OSGi modules. Don't worry, as you'll learn about them in an upcoming section of the chapter.

As Liferay's official documentation explains, "Service Builder is a model-driven code generation tool built by Liferay that allows developers to define custom object models called entities." Service Builder uses object-relational mapping (ORM) to generate a service layer. It provides a clear distinction between the object model and code for the database. These saves developers time in implementing those. It also offers built-in caching support (using `Ehcache`) to accelerate service execution. Service Builder lets developers use custom SQL and dynamic queries for any complex query depending on business logic. How ORM maps with relations is shown in Figure 5-1.

It is essential to understand that, even though Liferay provides a Service Builder, it's possible to use other Java-supported database persistence technologies, such as Hibernate.

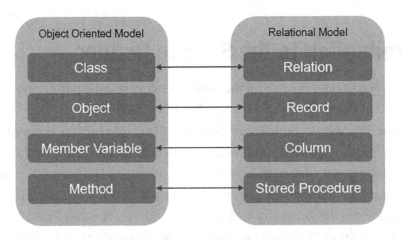

Figure 5-1. *ORM and relational model mapping*

This section has explained the basics of Service Builder; in the next section, you explore how to build services using Service Builder.

Generating Services

The first thing to understand is that Service Builder is a `service.xml` file. Using only this file, ORM is defined. You need to specify the entity names and fields, and then, when you build the service, the DAO layer is built.

By default, Liferay expects the `service.xml` file to reside in the root folder of the service module. However, it is customizable. In Service Builder taxonomy, model classes are referred to as *entities*. Let's look at how to create a Liferay Service Builder by using Liferay Developer Studio.

1. Open Liferay Developer Studio to the `apress_ws` workspace, which you used to create the Liferay portlets in Chapters 3 and 4. You use the same workspace so that all the Liferay-created code is in one place. Right-click the Modules folder and then choose New ➤ Liferay Module Project. (See Figure 5-2.)

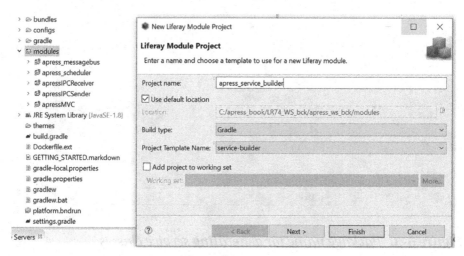

Figure 5-2. *Liferay Service Builder module creation*

2. Select Gradle for the build type, as you are building Gradle-based modules. (See Figure 5-2.)

3. Name the Project Template Name `service-builder`. This template will help you create a Liferay Service Builder. Click Next.

4. Once you click Finish, Developer Studio automatically creates your `apress service engine`, which will contain all the service-related classes and files. The `service.xml` file is the backbone of the Service Builder. (See Figure 5-3.)

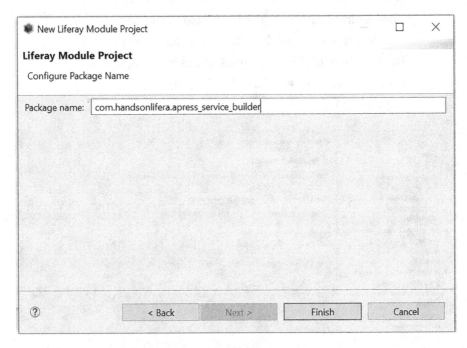

Figure 5-3. Package name for generating service classes

Let's look at the `service.xml` file you will use to understand this concept. It's shown in Listing 5-1. Update the `service.xml file` in the root directory of the service module. However, when you create the project,

there is a default service.xml file with default entries. You can also use
the GUI section to update service.xml from the Developer Studio, as
shown in Listing 5-1. Once you run the build-service, service.xml is
read by the Service Builder and the DAO layer is generated, as shown in
Listing 5-1.

Listing 5-1. Sample service.xml

```xml
<?xml version="1.0"?>
<!DOCTYPE service-builder PUBLIC "-//Liferay//DTD Service
Builder 7.4.0//EN" "http://www.liferay.com/dtd/liferay-service-
builder_7_4_0.dtd">

<service-builder dependency-injector="ds" package-path="com.
handsonliferay.apress_service_builder">
    <Author>Apoorva_Inthiyaz</author>
        <namespace>apress</namespace>

        <entity local-service="true" name="ApressBook" remote-
        service="true" uuid="true">

                <column name="bookId" primary="true"
                type="long" />

                <column name="groupId" type="long" />

                <column name="companyId" type="long" />
                <column name="chapterId" type="long" />
                <column name="chapterName" type="String" />
                <column name="createDate" type="Date" />
                <column name="isCoding" type="boolean" />

                <order by="asc">
                        <order-column name="chapterId" />
                </order>
```

```
<!-- Finder methods -->

<finder name="IsCoding" return-type="Collection">
        <finder-column name="isCoding" />
</finder>

<!-- References -->

<reference entity="AssetEntry" package-
path="com.liferay.portlet.asset" />
<reference entity="AssetTag" package-path="com.
liferay.portlet.asset" />
</entity>
<entity local-service="true" name="Emp" remote-
service="true" uuid="true">

        <column name="EmpId" primary="true"
        type="long" />

        <column name="groupId" type="long" />

        <column name="companyId" type="long" />
        <column name="projectId" type="long" />
        <column name="projectName" type="String" />
        <column name="createDate" type="Date" />
        <column name="isCoding" type="boolean" />

        <order by="asc">
                <order-column name="projectId" />
        </order>

        <!-- Finder methods -->

        <finder name="IsCoding" return-
        type="Collection">
                <finder-column name="isCoding" />
        </finder>
```

```
<!-- References -->

<reference entity="AssetEntry" package-
path="com.liferay.portlet.asset" />
<reference entity="AssetTag" package-path="com.
liferay.portlet.asset" />
    </entity>
</service-builder>
```

You can also use the GUI section to update service.xml from the Developer Studio, as shown in the following steps.

1. Define global information for the service. These settings are applied to all the services of the entities generated by this service.xml file. For example, package path, author, and so on, as shown in Figure 5-4.

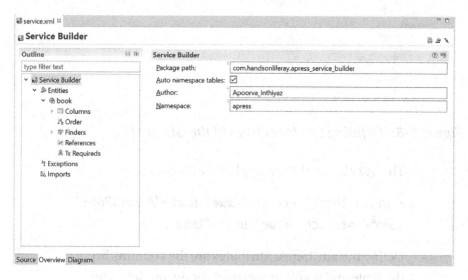

Figure 5-4. *GUI section to update service.xml*

2. These fields will appear as follows in service.xml:

```
<service-builder dependency-injector="ds"
package-path="com.handsonliferay.apress_
service_builder">
```

```
<Author>Apoorva_Inthiyaz</author>
<namespace>apress</namespace>
```

3. Define the service entities. Service entities are
    models in code and tables in the database. This is
    the first place where ORM starts taking place.
    (See Figure 5-5.)

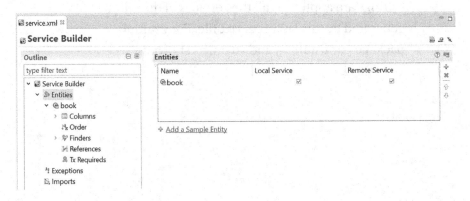

Figure 5-5. *Defining service entities in the GUI tool*

The service.xml file entry looks as follows:

```
<entity local-service="true" name="ApressBook"
remote-service="true" uuid="true">
```

4. Define the attributes. Attributes are the columns in
    the table and member variables for the models. This
    is the next step of ORM, as shown in Figure 5-6.

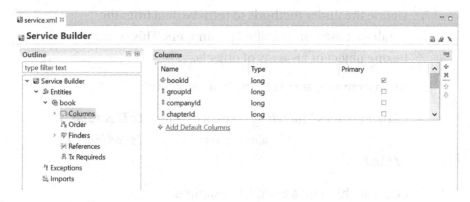

Figure 5-6. *Defining the attributes in the GUI tool*

The `service.xml` entry will look as follows:

```
<column name="bookId" primary="true" type="long" />

<column name="groupId" type="long" />

<column name="companyId" type="long" />
<column name="chapterId" type="long" />
<column name="chapterName" type="String" />
<column name="createDate" type="Date" />
<column name="isCoding" type="boolean" />
```

5. Define relationships between entities.

6. Define a default order for the data to be retrieved
    from the database, which can be ascending or
    descending. These are in the form of the entities.

    As an example, `service.xml` is shown here:

```
<order by="asc">
             <order-column name="chapterId" />
                    </order>
```

7.   Define the finder methods to retrieve data from the database based on specified parameters. This could be one object or an array of objects.

As an example, `service.xml` is shown here:

```
<finder name="IsCoding" return-type="Collection">
        <finder-column name="isCoding" />
</finder>
```

Let's review all this with a complete example.

You will generate service classes with the help of Gradle's Build Service task, which you can find in the following path. Go to the buildService tab by choosing Gradle Tasks ➤ apress_ws ➤ Module ➤ apress_service_builder ➤ apress_service_builder-service ➤ buildService. (See Figure 5-7.)

Figure 5-7. *Generate service classes*

160

In Figure 5-8, you can see all the service classes generated with the help of buildService. It will generate all the service-related classes—such as the wrappers, models, and utils—as well as the SQL and XML files required for the service layer.

Figure 5-8. *Console output of build service*

apress_service_builder contains two sub-modules. One is for the API classes and the other one is for service classes, as shown in Figure 5-9.

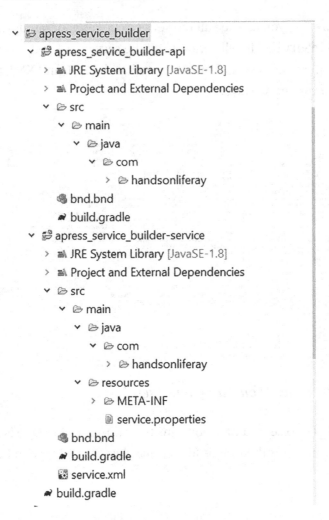

Figure 5-9. *Hierarchy of apress_service_builder*

Once you deploy `apress_service_builder` on the Liferay server, it will automatically create the tables shown in Figure 5-11, which are available in the entity section of `service.xml` with the `help tables.sql` file, as shown in Figure 5-10.

Figure 5-10. *SQL statement after building the service*

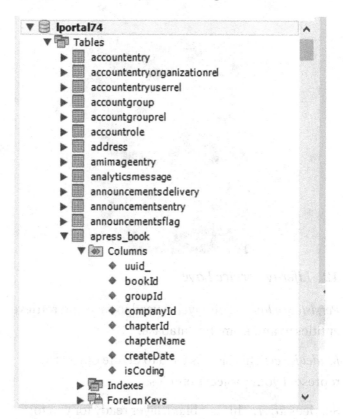

Figure 5-11. *Tables created in the database after deploying the service*

This section has explained how to build services using the Service Builder; in the next section, you learn about the code generated by the Service Builder.

Deep Diving Into the Code Generated by the Service Builder

By deep diving into the Liferay Service Builder, you will learn about the different layers of a Liferay service. You can understand this with the help of Figure 5-12.

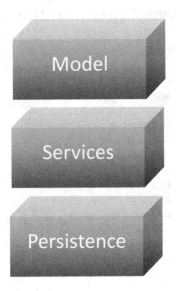

Figure 5-12. *Liferay Service Layer*

- *Persistence layer:* This layer is used to save and retrieve entities to and from the database.

- *Model layer:* This layer is used to define objects to represent your project's entities.

- Services *layer:* This is a blank layer ready for you to create your API and business logic.

Customization via Implementation Classes

Entity implementation: This is responsible for customizing the entity; all these classes will have the extension *Impl.Java.

Local service implementation: Local services are the core of the services generated by the Service Builder. As the name suggests, local services should be accessed by any class running in the same context. When you run the Service Builder, it is generated with the name of *LocalServiceImpl. This class is the entity's local service extension point. All the custom local services you need to write should be written in this class, but you need to access these classes from *LocalServiceUtil. The *LocalServiceUtil class contains only the signature of all the methods implemented in the LocalServiceImpl class, and these are registered in *LocalServiceUtil when you build the service. Whenever you add a new method or modify a method's parameter, you must build the service again. If it sounds complicated, check out the example in Listings 5-2 and 5-3.

Listing 5-2. ApressBookLocalServiceImpl Class

```
package com.handsonliferay.apress_service_builder.service.impl;

import com.handsonliferay.apress_service_builder.model.
ApressBook;
import com.handsonliferay.apress_service_builder.service.base.
ApressBookLocalServiceBaseImpl;

import com.liferay.portal.aop.AopService;

import java.util.Collection;

import org.osgi.service.component.annotations.Component;
/**
 * @author Apoorva_Inthiyaz
 */
```

```
@Component(
        property = "model.class.name=com.handsonliferay.apress_
        service_builder.model.ApressBook",
        service = AopService.class
)
public class ApressBookLocalServiceImpl extends
ApressBookLocalServiceBaseImpl {

}
```

Listing 5-3. ApressBookLocalServiceUtil Class

```
package com.handsonliferay.apress_service_builder.service;

import com.handsonliferay.apress_service_builder.model.
ApressBook;

import com.liferay.petra.sql.dsl.query.DSLQuery;
import com.liferay.portal.kernel.dao.orm.DynamicQuery;
import com.liferay.portal.kernel.exception.PortalException;
import com.liferay.portal.kernel.model.PersistedModel;
import com.liferay.portal.kernel.util.OrderByComparator;

import java.io.Serializable;

import java.util.List;
public class ApressBookLocalServiceUtil {
        public static ApressBook addApressBook(ApressBook
        apressBook) {
                return getService().addApressBook(apressBook);
        }
        public static ApressBook createApressBook(long bookId) {
                return getService().createApressBook(bookId);
        }
```

```java
public static PersistedModel createPersistedModel(
            Serializable primaryKeyObj)
    throws PortalException {

    return getService().createPersistedModel(primary
    KeyObj);
}
public static ApressBook deleteApressBook(ApressBook
apressBook) {
    return getService().deleteApressBook(apressBook);
}
public static ApressBook deleteApressBook(long bookId)
    throws PortalException {

    return getService().deleteApressBook(bookId);
}
public static PersistedModel deletePersistedModel(
            PersistedModel persistedModel)
    throws PortalException {

    return getService().deletePersistedModel
    (persistedModel);
}

public static <T> T dslQuery(DSLQuery dslQuery) {
    return getService().dslQuery(dslQuery);
}

public static int dslQueryCount(DSLQuery dslQuery) {
    return getService().dslQueryCount(dslQuery);
}

public static DynamicQuery dynamicQuery() {
    return getService().dynamicQuery();
}
```

```java
public static <T> List<T> dynamicQuery(DynamicQuery
dynamicQuery) {
        return getService().dynamicQuery(dynamicQuery);
}
public static <T> List<T> dynamicQuery(
        DynamicQuery dynamicQuery, int start,
        int end) {

        return getService().dynamicQuery(dynamicQuery,
        start, end);
}
public static <T> List<T> dynamicQuery(
        DynamicQuery dynamicQuery, int start, int end,
        OrderByComparator<T> orderByComparator) {

        return getService().dynamicQuery(
                dynamicQuery, start, end,
                orderByComparator);
}
public static long dynamicQueryCount(DynamicQuery
dynamicQuery) {
        return getService().dynamicQueryCount(dynamic
        Query);
}
public static long dynamicQueryCount(
        DynamicQuery dynamicQuery,
        com.liferay.portal.kernel.dao.orm.Projection
        projection) {

        return getService().
        dynamicQueryCount(dynamicQuery, projection);
}
```

```
public static ApressBook fetchApressBook(long bookId) {
    return getService().fetchApressBook(bookId);
}
public static ApressBook fetchApressBookByUuidAndGroupId(
        String uuid, long groupId) {

    return getService().fetchApressBookByUuidAnd
    GroupId(uuid, groupId);
}

public static java.util.Collection<ApressBook>
findByisCoding(
        Boolean iscode) {

    return getService().findByisCoding(iscode);
}

public static com.liferay.portal.kernel.dao.orm.
ActionableDynamicQuery
        getActionableDynamicQuery() {

    return getService().
    getActionableDynamicQuery();
}
public static ApressBook getApressBook(long bookId)
throws PortalException {
    return getService().getApressBook(bookId);
}
public static ApressBook getApressBookByUuidAndGroupId(
                String uuid, long groupId)
        throws PortalException {

    return getService().getApressBookByUuidAndGroup
    Id(uuid, groupId);
}
```

```java
public static List<ApressBook> getApressBooks(int
start, int end) {
        return getService().getApressBooks(start, end);
}
public static List<ApressBook>
getApressBooksByUuidAndCompanyId(
        String uuid, long companyId) {

        return getService().getApressBooksByUuidAnd
        CompanyId(uuid, companyId);
}
public static List<ApressBook>
getApressBooksByUuidAndCompanyId(
        String uuid, long companyId, int start, int end,
        OrderByComparator<ApressBook> orderByComparator) {

        return getService().
        getApressBooksByUuidAndCompanyId(
                uuid, companyId, start, end,
                orderByComparator);
}
public static int getApressBooksCount() {
        return getService().getApressBooksCount();
}

public static
        com.liferay.portal.kernel.dao.orm.
        IndexableActionableDynamicQuery
                getIndexableActionableDynamicQuery() {

        return getService().
        getIndexableActionableDynamicQuery();
}
```

```java
public static String getOSGiServiceIdentifier() {
        return getService().getOSGiServiceIdentifier();
}
public static PersistedModel
getPersistedModel(Serializable primaryKeyObj)
        throws PortalException {

        return getService().getPersistedModel(primary
        KeyObj);
}
public static ApressBook updateApressBook(ApressBook
apressBook) {
        return getService().
        updateApressBook(apressBook);
}

public static ApressBookLocalService getService() {
        return _service;
}

private static volatile ApressBookLocalService _
service;
}
```

Remote Service Implementation

You already know what a local service is. A remote service, on the other hand, is a service that can be accessed from resources running outside of the application context. Liferay DXP allows you to expose web services as JSON and SOAP web services. Even various Liferay services are available in the form of web services.

You can list JSON services using the following URL on your development environment:

```
http://localhost:8080/api/jsonws/
```

You can list SOAP web services using the following URL on your development environment:

```
http://localhost:8080/api/axis
```

To generate remote services for your custom entities, you must run the Service Builder with the remote-service attribute set to true. After setting this, you need to build the service again, which will generate all the classes, interfaces, and files required to support SOAP and JSON web services. Once the service is built, it provides *ServiceImpl, as shown in Listing 5-4, where you need to write the business logic for implementing remote services. The best practice when implementing a remote service is to add a proper permission check because remotes services are open for access from other applications.

Another best practice is to implement the business logic in *LocalServiceImpl and invoke it from *ServiceImpl after doing the permission check. Listing 5-4 shows an example.

Listing 5-4. ApressBookLocalServiceUtil Class

```
package com.handsonliferay.apress_service_builder.service.impl;

import com.handsonliferay.apress_service_builder.service.base.
ApressBookServiceBaseImpl;

import com.liferay.portal.aop.AopService;

import org.osgi.service.component.annotations.Component;

/**
 * @author Apoorva_Inthiyaz
 */
```

```
@Component(
        property = {
                "json.web.service.context.name=apress",
                "json.web.service.context.path=ApressBook"
        },
        service = AopService.class
)
public class ApressBookServiceImpl extends
ApressBookServiceBaseImpl {
}
```

CRUD Operations

CRUD (Create, Read, Update and Delete) operations are used when interacting with persistent storage. They are defined as follows:

- **Create**: The Create operation is an INSERT operation in SQL. A new value is inserted into the database.

- **Read**: The Read operation is a SELECT operation in SQL. Values are fetched from the database. You'll see this in detail in the "Finder" section of this chapter.

- **Update**: The Update operation is an UPDATE operation in SQL. Inserted values can be modified.

- **Delete**: The Delete operation is DELETE in SQL. You can delete the existing values from the database.

Let's see how these are implemented. To use these services in any module, you need to add dependencies to the build. The Gradle file of the consumer module is shown in Listing 5-5. The apressMVC module has been added, which was created in Chapter 2.

Listing 5-5. Adding Service Builder Dependencies to the build.
gradle File

```
dependencies {
        compileOnly group: "com.liferay.portal", name:
        "release.dxp.api"

        compileOnly project(":modules:apress_service_
        builder:apress_service_builder-api")
        compileOnly project(":modules:apress_service_
        builder:apress_service_builder-service")

        cssBuilder group: "com.liferay", name: "com.liferay.
        css.builder", version: "3.0.2"
}
```

compileOnly project(":modules:apress_service_builder:apress_
service_builder-api") is used in the build.gradle file, which enables
apress_service_builder-api classes to be available to the apressMVC
portlet.

compileOnly project(":modules:apress_service_builder:apress_
service_builder-service") is used in the build.gradle file, which
enables apress_service_builder-service classes to be available.

The example code in Listing 5-6 creates an entry in a table using
Liferay Service Builder services.

Listing 5-6. Code Snippet to Create an Entry in a Custom Table

```
import com.apress.handsonliferay.constants.
ApressMVCPortletKeys;
import com.handsonliferay.apress_service_builder.model.
ApressBook;
import com.handsonliferay.apress_service_builder.model.impl.
ApressBookImpl;
```

```
import com.handsonliferay.apress_service_builder.service.
ApressBookLocalServiceUtil;
                ApressBook apressBook = new ApressBookImpl();
                    apressBook.setBookId(CounterLocalServic
                    eUtil.increment());
                    apressBook.setChapterName("Liferay");
                    apressBook.setCreateDate(new Date());
                    apressBook.setIsCoding(true);
                ApressBookLocalServiceUtil.addApressBook(ap
                ressBook);
```

Listing 5-7 shows example code that updates the table entry created using Liferay Service Builder services. This example is updating the chapter name HandsOnliferay to an entry whose bookId is 1234.

Listing 5-7. Code Snippet to Update an Entry in a Custom Table

```
ApressBook apressBook1 = ApressBookLocalServiceUtil.fetchApress
Book(1234);
                    apressBook1.setChapterName("HandsOnliferay");
ApressBookLocalServiceUtil.updateApressBook(apressBook1);
```

Listing 5-8 shows example code that deletes an entry from the table created by using Liferay Service Builder services. This example is deleting the entry with its bookId set to 1234 in two different ways.

Listing 5-8. Code Snippet to Delete an Entry in a Custom Table

```
// Way 1
ApressBookLocalServiceUtil.deleteApressBook(1234);

// Way 2
ApressBook apressBookOb = ApressBookLocalServiceUtil.fetchApres
sBook(1234);
ApressBookLocalServiceUtil.deleteApressBook(apressBookOb);
```

Listing 5-9 shows example code that reads an entry from the table created using Liferay Service Builder services. This example reads the entry with a bookId of 1234.

Listing 5-9. Code Snippet to Read an Entry from a Custom Table

```
ApressBook apressBook = ApressBookLocalServiceUtil.fetchApress
Book(1234);
System.out.println(" Book name :"+ apressBook.getChapterName();
```

Finders

Liferay Service Builder provides a straightforward approach for fetching data from database table columns. These methods are called *finder methods*. They are easy to implement but have a drawback: they are fit for simple fetch operations, not for complex ones. To generate a finder method, you must add a finder tag to the `service.xml` file and configure it accordingly.

Data retrieved by the finder methods is in the form of model objects that fulfill the specified criteria. The Service Builder generates several methods based on each finder created for an entity. It creates methods to fetch, find, remove, and count entity instances based on the finder's parameters.

Let's see this concept with an example:

1.   Write a `service.xml` file (see Listing 5-10).

Listing 5-10. Writing a Finder in Service.xml

```
<service-builder dependency-injector="ds" package-path="com.
handsonliferay.apress_service_builder">
    <Author>Apoorva_Inthiyaz</author>
        <namespace>apress</namespace>
```

```
<entity local-service="true" name="ApressBook" remote-
service="true" uuid="true">

        <column name="bookId" primary="true"
        type="long" />

        <column name="groupId" type="long" />

        <column name="companyId" type="long" />
        <column name="chapterId" type="long" />
        <column name="chapterName" type="String" />
        <column name="createDate" type="Date" />
        <column name="isCoding" type="boolean" />

        <order by="asc">
                <order-column name="chapterId" />
        </order>

        <!-- Finder methods -->

        <finder name="IsCoding" return-
        type="Collection">
                <finder-column name="isCoding" />
        </finder>

        <!-- References -->

        <reference entity="AssetEntry" package-
        path="com.liferay.portlet.asset" />
        <reference entity="AssetTag" package-path="com.
        liferay.portlet.asset" />
    </entity>
</service-builder>
```

2.   Write the business logic for the custom finder in the
     Entity Local Service Impl class.

3.   After these changes, you need to add buildService
     to the Service Builder module. (See Listing 5-11.)

Listing 5-11. Writing Finder Business Logic in the
ApressBookLocalServiceImpl Class

```
package com.handsonliferay.apress_service_builder.service.impl;

import com.handsonliferay.apress_service_builder.model.
ApressBook;
import com.handsonliferay.apress_service_builder.service.base.
ApressBookLocalServiceBaseImpl;

import com.liferay.portal.aop.AopService;

import java.util.Collection;

import org.osgi.service.component.annotations.Component;
/**
 * @author Apoorva_Inthiyaz
 */
@Component(
        property = "model.class.name=com.handsonliferay.apress_
service_builder.model.ApressBook",
        service = AopService.class
)
public class ApressBookLocalServiceImpl extends
ApressBookLocalServiceBaseImpl {

        public Collection<ApressBook> findByisCoding(Boolean
        iscode){
```

```
        return apressBookPersistence.
        findByIsCoding(iscode);
    }

}
```

4. Invoke the custom implemented finder in the custom module (see Listing 5-12).

Listing 5-12. Invoking the Custom Implemented Finder

```
Collection<ApressBook> apressBookObj = ApressBookLocalService
Util.findByisCoding(false);
```

Dynamic Query

Liferay allows custom SQL queries to retrieve data from the database. However, in real-world applications, you'll need to build queries dynamically. (If you do not want to build the query dynamically, you can use Custom SQL, which you'll see in the next section.) Returning to dynamic queries, Liferay provides the DynamicQuery API. The DynamicQuery API is a wrapper of the Hibernates Criteria API.

When creating a dynamic query, a SQL query is generated by the code using the DynamicQuery API, where you write Java code, not SQL. In the DynamicQuery API, the query is written as Java code, where variables and objects are used instead of tables and columns. These queries are simple to write and implement in comparison to SQL queries.

Listing 5-13 shows an example. This example uses a dynamic query to fetch all the users from a database table called user.

Listing 5-13. Dynamic Query Code Snippet for a Custom Table

```
import com.liferay.portal.kernel.dao.orm.DynamicQuery;
import com.liferay.portal.kernel.dao.orm.
DynamicQueryFactoryUtil;
import com.liferay.portal.kernel.dao.orm.
RestrictionsFactoryUtil;
DynamicQuery userQuery = DynamicQueryFactoryUtil.forClass(User.
class, "user",

                                PortalClassLoaderUtil.
                                getClassLoader());
                    userQuery.add(RestrictionsFactoryUtil.l
                    ike("user.emailAddress", "test%"));
                    try {
                            List<User> customUsersList = Us
                            erLocalServiceUtil.dynamicQuery
                            (userQuery);
                            for (User user :
                            customUsersList) {
                                    System.out.println("ID:
                                    " + user.getUserId() +
                                    " Name: " + user.
                                    getFirstName() +
                                    " Email ID: " + user.
                                    getEmailAddress());
                            }
                    } catch (SystemException e) {

                    }
```

Custom SQL

The Service Builder generates finder methods that fetch values for the tables. You learned about finders and dynamic queries in the previous sections. Real-world applications are sometimes too complex to be covered by simple finders and dynamic queries. In those cases, custom SQL is implemented.

Custom SQL gives you the liberty to directly execute SQL statements for implementation, but great power comes with great responsibility. Custom SQL comes with the drawback—if the application's database changes, you may have to modify the query based on the database engine's query syntax. For instance, if you were using MySQL as a portal database (so all the custom SQL is written in MySQL) and then later you move the database to Oracle, the Custom SQL queries need to be modified according to the Oracle syntax. More complex cases such as joins are the major cases where these are implemented. You learn how to implement Custom SQL in this tutorial.

Liferay custom SQL is supported by the Service Builder method. It helps execute custom complex queries against the database by invoking custom SQL from a finder method in your persistence layer. The Service Builder enables you to generate these interfaces in your finder method.

Follow these steps to do this:

1. Specify your Custom SQL.

   You need to specify it in a particular file so Liferay can access it. The `CustomSQLUtil` class (from the `com.liferay.portal.dao.orm.custom.sql` module) retrieves the SQL from a file called `default.xml` in your service module's `src/main/resources/META-INF/custom-sql/` folder. You must create the `custom-sql` folder and a `default.xml` file in that `custom-sql` folder. The `default.xml` file must adhere to the format shown in Listing 5-14.

Listing 5-14. The default.xml File for the Custom SQL

```
<custom-sql>
<sql id="com.apress.handsonliferay.service.persistence.
EntryFinder.findByApressbookName">
<![CDATA[
 SELECT AP_Entry.*
    FROM AP_Entry INNER JOIN
AP_Apressbook ON AP_Entry.bookId = AP_Apressbook.bookId
 WHERE (AP_Entry.name LIKE ?) AND (AP_Apressbook.name LIKE ?)
]]>
</sql></custom-sql>
```

2. Implement your custom finder method.

    Service Builder generates the interface for the
    finder in your API module. Still, you have to
    create the implementation to implement the
    finder method in the persistence layer to invoke
    your custom SQL query. First, you need to create
    a *FinderImpl class in the service persistence
    package. In the Apressbook application, you
    could create an EntryFinderImpl class in the com.
    apress.handsonliferay.service.persistence.
    impl package. Your class should extend
    BasePersistenceImpl<Entry>.

    Run the Service Builder to generate the *Finder
    interface based on the *FinderImpl class. Modify
    your *FinderImpl class to make it a component
    (annotated with @Component) that implements
    the *Finder interface you just generated. (See
    Listing 5-15.)

Listing 5-15. EntryFinderImpl for the Custom SQL

```java
@Component(service = EntryFinder.class)
public class EntryFinderImpl extends BasePersistenceImpl<Event>
    implements EntryFinder {

        public List<Entry> findByApressbookName(
                String entryName, String entryMessage,
                String guestbookName,
                int begin, int end) {

                Session session = null;
                try {
                    session = openSession();

                    String sql = CustomSQLUtil.get(
                        getClass(),
                        FIND_BY_ENTRYNAME_BOOKNAME);

                    SQLQuery q = session.createSQLQuery(sql);
                    q.setCacheable(false);
                    q.addEntity("AP_Entry",
                    EntryImpl.class);

                    QueryPos qPos = QueryPos.
                    getInstance(q);
                    qPos.add(entryName);
                    qPos.add(entryMessage);
                    qPos.add(guestbookName);

                    return (List<Entry>) QueryUtil.list(q,
                    getDialect(), begin, end);
                }
```

```
            catch (Exception e) {
                try {
                    throw new SystemException(e);
                }
                catch (SystemException se) {
                    se.printStackTrace();
                }
            }
            finally {
                closeSession(session);
            }

            return null;
        }

        public static final String FIND_BY_ENTRYNAME_
        BOOKNAME =
            EntryFinder.class.getName() +
                ".findByApressbookName";
}
```

3. Access your finder method from the service.

```
public List<Entry> findByApressbookName(String entryName,
        String bookName) throws SystemException {

        return entryFinder.findByApressbookName(String
        entryName,
            String bookName);
    }
```

Working with Remote Services

Now that you understand how to create a service and consume it in your controller class, there is another type that can be consumed from other applications as well. These services are referred to as *remote services*. They come in handy when you need your application to communicate with other applications of ecology. Liferay provides features to expose services as remote components that are straightforward and easy to maintain. Liferay offers two approaches to achieve this, discussed in the following sections.

Headless REST APIs

As their name suggests, these services are not consumed in the application exposing the services. In a way, your application works as a microservice host, a new-age way of working with APIs. These services are RESTful web services, independent of Liferay DXP's front-end. This is why they are called headless. These APIs fulfill the OpenAPI specification.

Liferay DXP's headless REST APIs leverage OpenAPI (known initially as Swagger); you don't need a service catalog. You only need to know the OpenAPI profile to discover the rest of the APIs to begin consuming the web service.

Liferay DXP's headless APIs are available in SwaggerHub at https:// app.swaggerhub.com/organizations/liferayinc.

Each API has its own URL in SwaggerHub.

For example, you can access the delivery API definition at https:// app.swaggerhub.com/apis/liferayinc/headless-delivery/v1.0.

Each OpenAPI profile is also deployed dynamically in your portal instance under this schema:

http://[host]:[port]/o/[insert-headless-api]/[version]/ openapi.yaml

For example, if you're running Liferay DXP locally on port 8080, the home URL for discovering the headless delivery API is:

```
http://localhost:8080/o/headless-delivery/v1.0/openapi.yaml
```

You must be logged in to access this URL or use basic authentication and a browser. You can also use other tools like Postman, an advanced REST client, or even the `curl` command from your system console.

Run this `curl` command to access the home URL:

```
curl http://localhost:8080/o/headless-delivery/v1.0/openapi.
yaml -u test@liferay.com:test
```

For example, to invoke specific site blog posting details, you use the following snippet:

```
curl "http://localhost:8080/o/headless-delivery/v1.0/
sites/20124/blog-postings/" -u 'test@liferay.com:test'
```

Let's look at this process in more detail with an example. You will use Blade to create this example.

1. Create a project using Blade, as follows:

   ```
   blade init -v 7.2 books
   ```

2. Edit this project's `build.gradle` file to get the REST builder Gradle plugin. The REST builder Gradle plugin lets you generate a REST layer that's defined in the REST builder's `rest-config.yaml` and `rest-openapi.yaml` files. To use this plugin, include it in your build script, as shown in Listing 5-16.

Listing 5-16. The Build Script

```
buildscript {
    dependencies {
        classpath group: "com.liferay", name: "com.liferay.
        gradle.plugins.rest.builder", version: "1.0.21"
    }

    repositories {
        maven {
            url "https://repository-cdn.liferay.com/nexus/
            content/groups/public"
        }
    }
}

apply plugin: "com.liferay.portal.tools.rest.builder"
```

The REST builder plugin automatically resolves the Liferay REST builder library as a dependency; you have to configure a repository that hosts the library and its transitive dependencies.

```
repositories {
    maven {
        url "https://repository-cdn.liferay.com/nexus/content/
        groups/public"
    }
}
```

This plugin will add one task to the buildREST project. By default, the REST builder plugin creates a configuration called restBuilder and adds a dependency to its most recent version.

```
dependencies {
    restBuilder group: "com.liferay", name: "com.liferay.
    portal.tools.rest.builder", version: "1.0.22"
}
```

3. Quickly check the tasks by using ./gradlew tasks
   from the command prompt to the books project.
   The output is shown in Listing 5-17.

Listing 5-17. Execution of the Gradle Tasks Command

```
$ ./gradlew tasks

> Task :tasks

------------------------------------------------------------------
All tasks runnable from the root project
------------------------------------------------------------------

Build tasks
-----------
assemble - Assembles the outputs of this project.
build - Assembles and tests this project.
buildCSS - Build CSS files.
buildDependents - Assembles and tests this project and all
projects that depend on it.
buildLang - Runs Liferay Lang Builder to translate language
property files.
buildNeeded - Assembles and tests this project and all projects
it depends on.
buildREST - Runs Liferay REST Builder.
```

4. Create a handful of modules.

```
$ cd modules/headless-books
$ blade create -t api -v 7.2 -p com.apress.handsonliferay.
headless.books headless-books-api
Successfully created project headless-books-api in books/
modules/headless-books
$ blade create -t api -v 7.2 -p com.apress.handsonliferay.
headless.books headless-books-impl
Successfully created project headless-books-impl in books/
modules/headless-books
$ blade create -t api -v 7.2 -p com.apress.handsonliferay.
headless.books headless-books-client
Successfully created project headless-books-client in books/
modules/headless-books
$ blade create -t api -v 7.2 -p com.apress.handsonliferay.
headless.books headless-books-test
Successfully created project headless-books-test in books/
modules/headless-books
```

5. Create the YAML files that will define the service
   endpoints. To headless-books-impl, you need to add
   the rest-config.yaml file, as shown in Listing 5-18.
   The rest-openapi.yaml file must also be created in
   your headless-books-impl module.

Listing 5-18. The rest-config.yaml File

```
apiDir: "../headless-books-api/src/main/java"
apiPackagePath: " com.apress.handsonliferay.headless.books"
application:
    baseURI: "/headless-books"
    className: "HeadlessBooksApplication"
    name: "Apress.Handsonliferay.Headless.Books"
```

```
author: "Apoorva_Inthiyaz"
clientDir: "../headless-books-client/src/main/java"
testDir: "../headless-books-test/src/testIntegration/java"
```

Every OpenAPI YAML file has three sections: meta, paths (endpoints), and reusable components (type definitions), and these files are no different; see Listings 5-19 and 5-20.

Listing 5-19. The Meta Section of the File

```
openapi: 3.0.1
info:
  title: "Headless Books"
  version: v1.0
  description: "API for accessing Book details."
```

Listing 5-20. Reusable Components

```
components:
  schemas:
    Book:
      description: Contains all of the data for a single book.
      properties:
        name:
          description: The book name.
          type: string
        id:
          description: The book ID.
          type: string
        chapterNames:
          description: The Chapter names of the book.
           type: string
```

```
creator:
    $ref: "#/components/schemas/Creator"
type: object
```

In YAML file indents signify depth, so a line at a higher indent is a child, and a line at the same depth is a sibling. The creator is a reference to another object in the file (that's $ref). When you do have a $ref in the same file, it means you need to include the reference.

Plain Web/REST Services

This is the legacy way to build and consume web services in Liferay DXP, but it is still supported. This lets you use JAX-RS, JAX-WS, or the Service Builder to implement plain REST or SOAP web services. You learned how to implement these services in a previous section of this chapter, where implementation of web service is explained.

When you build services with the Service Builder, all remote-enabled services (i.e., service.xml entities with remote-service="true") are exposed as JSON web services. This is shown in the following snippet:

```
<entity local-service="true" name="ApressBook" remote-
service="true" uuid="true">
```

To test Liferay's JSON web service registration process, add a simple method to your Apress services. Edit your ApressBookServiceImpl class as shown in Listing 5-21.

Listing 5-21. ApressBookServiceImpl with a Custom Method

```
package com.handsonliferay.apress_service_builder.service.impl;

import com.handsonliferay.apress_service_builder.service.base.
ApressBookServiceBaseImpl;

import com.liferay.portal.aop.AopService;
```

```java
import org.osgi.service.component.annotations.Component;

/**
 * @author Apoorva_Inthiyaz
 */
@Component(
        property = {
                "json.web.service.context.name=apress",
                "json.web.service.context.path=ApressBook"
        },
        service = AopService.class
)
public class ApressBookServiceImpl extends
ApressBookServiceBaseImpl {

        public String helloWorld(String worldName) {
            return "Hello world: " + worldName;
        }
}
```

Rebuild the services and redeploy your app's modules. You can now invoke this service method via JSON.

You can create the mapped URL of an exposed service by following this naming convention:

```
http://[server]:[port]/api/jsonws/[context-path].[service-
class-name]/[service-method-name]
```

[context-path], [service-class-name] ,[service-method-name] is defined in your *ServiceImpl. Note in Listing 5-21 that the following snippet is used:

```
property = {
                "json.web.service.context.name=apress",
                "json.web.service.context.path=ApressBook"
        },
```

This snippet calls the hello-world method:

```
http://localhost:8080/api/jsonws/apress.ApressBook/hello-world
```

Listing 5-22 provides different ways of creating these URLs by different annotation values.

Listing 5-22. ApressBookServiceImpl with the addBook Method Ways

```
package com.handsonliferay.apress_service_builder.service.impl;

import com.handsonliferay.apress_service_builder.service.base.
ApressBookServiceBaseImpl;
import com.liferay.portal.aop.AopService;
import com.liferay.portal.kernel.jsonwebservice.JSONWebService;

import org.osgi.service.component.annotations.Component;

/**
 * @author Apoorva_Inthiyaz
 */
@Component(
        property = {
                "json.web.service.context.name=apress",
                "json.web.service.context.path=ApressBook"
        },
        service = AopService.class
)
```

```
@JSONWebService("abs")
public class ApressBookServiceImpl extends
ApressBookServiceBaseImpl {

        public String helloWorld(String worldName) {
            return "Hello world: " + worldName;
        }

        @JSONWebService(value = "add-book-wow", method = "PUT")
        public boolean addBook() {
                return false;
        }

        @JSONWebService("/add-something-very-specific")
        public boolean addApressBook() {
                return true;
        }
}
```

This concludes how a service can be exposed from Liferay DXP.

Summary

In this chapter, you learned about the easiest way to create a service and DAO layer for a portlet, which is using the Service Builder. The Service Builder uses the service.xml file to generate the ORM and its methods. You can do CRUD operations using these generated methods. To perform CRUD operations, local and remote services can be used. Local and remote services can be invoked, depending on the context in which the service is being invoked. To fetch data from tables, you can implement finders, dynamic queries, or Custom SQL, depending on the complexity of the query.

In the next chapter, you will go through different ways of customizing Liferay DXP.

CHAPTER 6

Liferay Customization

Portlets are the main component when it comes to creating any portal. Liferay is no different. Themes are developed to give these portlets headers and footers so they have a project-specific look and feel. But what if you have an out-of-box Liferay DXP portlet that matches your requirements, and a minor tweak can make it serve your project-specific business needs? What should you do in that case? To address this scenario, Liferay DXP provides an approach to customize behavior. These customizations range from simple JSP changes and extensions to a level where you can modify the overall behavior of the Liferay DXP portal. This chapter explains how it's done.

Overriding Language Keys

Internationalization (i18n) and localization can be achieved quickly in Liferay, by using language property files. Language property files are nothing but resource bundles with key and value pairs. These values are replaced when the key is found in the implemented code at runtime. These property files can be used in custom portlets as well. There are two types of languages that can be modified: global language properties and module language properties. The following sections discuss both.

© Apoorva Prakash and Shaik Inthiyaz Basha 2022
A. Prakash and S. I. Basha, *Hands- On Liferay DXP*,
https://doi.org/10.1007/978-1-4842-8563-3_6

Global Language Property

Say you need to replace the word "user" across the portal with the word "employee." This is an example of a global language property. To do this, you need to create a resource bundle service component.

The following example illustrates this concept.

1. Determine the language keys to override. You need to determine the keys that you want to override from the source in the /portal-impl/src/content/ Language[xx_XX].properties path from a portal-impl.jar bundle. For example: lang.user.name. required.field.names=Required-Last-Name.

2. Override the keys in a new language properties file. Listing 6-1 shows how to change the lang.user. name.required.field.names key value from last-name to Required-Last-Name.

3. Create a resource bundle service component, as shown in Listing 6-1.

Listing 6-1. ResourceBundle Class

```
package com.apress.handsonliferay.portlet;

import com.liferay.portal.kernel.language.UTF8Control;

import java.util.Enumeration;
import java.util.ResourceBundle;

import org.osgi.service.component.annotations.Component;

/**
 * @author Inthiyaz_Apoorva
 */
```

```
@Component(
            property = { "language.id=en_US" },
            service = ResourceBundle.class
)
public class RosourceBundlePortlet extends ResourceBundle {

        @Override
        protected Object handleGetObject(String key) {
                return _resourceBundle.getObject(key);
        }

        @Override
        public Enumeration<String> getKeys() {
                return _resourceBundle.getKeys();
        }

        private final ResourceBundle _resourceBundle =
                        ResourceBundle.getBundle("content.
                        Language_en_US", UTF8Control.INSTANCE);
}
```

The @Component annotation shown in Listing 6-1 declares it an OSGi ResourceBundle service component. Its language.id property designates it for the en_US locale.

```
@Component(
property = { "language.id=en_US" },
service = ResourceBundle.class
)
```

The code shown in Listing 6-2 is helpful for illustrating resource bundle assignment.

Listing 6-2. Resource Bundle Assignment

```
private final ResourceBundle _resourceBundle =
ResourceBundle.getBundle("content.Language_en_US",
UTF8Control.INSTANCE);
```

Module Language Property

To customize a module's language property, you need to create and prioritize the module's resource bundle.

Let's look at this more closely with an example.

1. Find the module and its metadata and language keys. As shown in Figures 6-1 and 6-2, you will use the Gogo shell to achieve this. Choose Control Panel ➤ Gogo Shell.

Gogo Shell

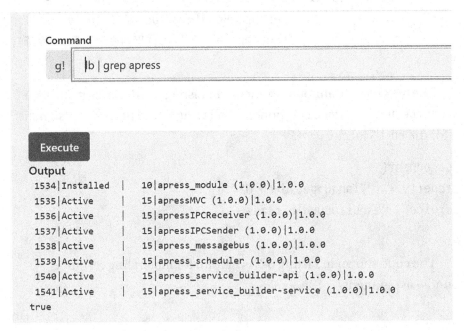

Figure 6-1. *Gogo shell's lb command*

Gogo Shell

g! | headers 1535

Execute

Output
```
Bundle headers:
 Bnd-LastModified = 1650643756190
 Bundle-ManifestVersion = 2
 Bundle-Name = apressMVC
 Bundle-SymbolicName = com.apress.handsonliferay
 Bundle-Version = 1.0.0
 Created-By = 1.8.0_181 (Oracle Corporation)
 Export-Package = com.apress.handsonliferay.constants;version="1.0.0"
 Import-Package = com.liferay.portal.kernel.portlet,com.liferay.portal.kernel.portlet.bridges.mvc,
 Javac-Debug = on
 Javac-Deprecation = off
 Javac-Encoding = Cp1252
 Manifest-Version = 1.0
 Private-Package = com.apress.handsonliferay.portlet,content
 Provide-Capability = osgi.service;objectClass:List<String>="com.liferay.portal.kernel.portlet.bri
 Require-Capability = osgi.extender;filter:="(&(osgi.extender=jsp.taglib)(uri=http://java.sun.com/
 Service-Component = OSGI-INF/com.apress.handsonliferay.portlet.ApressMVCActionCommand.xml,OSGI-IN
 Tool = Bnd-5.2.0.202010142003
```

Figure 6-2. *Gogo shell's headers command*

2. In Figure 6-2, note the bundle symbolic name and the servlet context name and version. You'll use these to create the resource bundle loader later in the process.

   For example, here are those for the Liferay Blogs Web module:

   Bundle symbolic name: com.apress.handsonliferay
   Bundle version: 1.0.0

3. Next, find the module's JAR file so you can examine its language keys. Then write your custom language key values. To achieve this, you need to write a new module to hold a resource bundle loader

and keys. In that module's path, within the `src/`
`main/resources/content` *folder*, create language
properties files for the locale whose keys you want to
override. In the language properties file, specify your
language key overrides.

4.   Prioritize your module's resource bundle. Now that
your language keys are in place, use OSGi manifest
headers to specify the language keys for the target
module. To compliment the target module's
resource bundle, you'll aggregate your resource
bundle with the target module's resource bundle.
You'll list your module first to prioritize its resource
bundle over the target module resource bundle.

This section has explained how language keys are modified. In the next
section, you see how to customize JSPs.

Customizing JSPs

Customizing JSPs is the basic customization process in Liferay. This
lets you modify the existing JSPs of the Liferay portal and any out-of-
box portlets. Customizing JSPs lets developers leverage the out-of-the-
box Liferay DXP functionality and customize them based on business
requirements. This results in minimizing development efforts. There are
two approaches for JSPs customization, using Liferay APIs and overriding
a JSP using an OSGi fragment. They are both discussed in the following
sections.

Customization JSPs with Liferay APIs

There are various approaches to customizing portlets and Liferay core JSPs; out of them, Liferay DXP's API approach is considered the easiest and best. Even the Liferay official documentation highly recommends the API-based approach. This can be achieved with one of the methods discussed in the following sections.

Dynamic Includes

As the name suggests, this approach adds contents dynamically, which works with the help of dynamic include tags. This is easy to implement and fits where you need to add more code to the existing JSPs. However, it comes with a limitation: its usage is limited to the JSPs that use dynamic-include tags or classes that inherit IncludeTag. Every JSP contains a placeholder liferay-util:dynamic-include tag, which is an extension point for inserting content such as HTML and JavaScript. There are cases when this placeholder is not present in JSPs; in such instances, you need to use another customization approach.

The code examples in Listings 6-3 and 6-4 show how to achieve this approach. Add extra compile-only dependencies to the build file of the newly created custom module.

Listing 6-3. The Build File for Dynamic Include

```
dependencies {
        compileOnly group: "com.liferay.portal", name:
        "release.dxp.api"

        cssBuilder group: "com.liferay", name: "com.liferay.
        css.builder", version: "3.0.2"
```

```
        compileOnly group: "javax.portlet", name: "portlet-
        api", version: "2.0"
        compileOnly group: "javax.servlet", name: "javax.
        servlet-api", version: "3.0.1"
        compileOnly group: "com.liferay", name: "com.liferay.
        petra.string", version: "1.0.0"
        compileOnly group: "com.liferay. ", name: "com.liferay.
        portal.kernel", version: "2.0.0"
        compileOnly group: "org.osgi", name: "osgi.cmpn",
        version: "6.0.0"
}
```

Listing 6-4. Dynamic Include Implementation Class

```
package com.apress.handsonliferay.portlet;

import com.liferay.portal.kernel.servlet.taglib.DynamicInclude;

import java.io.IOException;
import java.io.PrintWriter;

import javax.servlet.http.HttpServletRequest;
import javax.servlet.http.HttpServletResponse;

import org.osgi.service.component.annotations.Component;

/**
 * @author Inthiyaz_Apoorva
 */
@Component(
            immediate = true,
            service = DynamicInclude.class
    )
```

```java
public class MyBlogsDynamicIncludePortlet implements
DynamicInclude {

        @Override
        public void include(
                        HttpServletRequest request,
                        HttpServletResponse response,
                        String key)
                throws IOException {
                PrintWriter printWriter = response.getWriter();
                printWriter.println("<h2>Added by Blogs Dynamic
                Include!</h2><br />");
        }

        @Override
        public void register(DynamicIncludeRegistry
        dynamicIncludeRegistry) {
                dynamicIncludeRegistry.register(
                        "com.liferay.blogs.web#/blogs/view_
                        entry.jsp#pre");
        }
}
```

The DynamicInclude interface implementation is shown in Listing 6-4, and it contains the include() and register() methods. By overriding these methods, you can achieve this functionality.

Portlet Filters

Using this approach, a JSP is not modified directly; instead, the portlet request and response are modified to simulate the customization. Before a portlet request or response is processed, the filter intercepts and modifies it. The main advantage of portlet filters is that they provide access to alter the JSP's complete content, unlike a dynamic include, where you can append some content.

Listing 6-5 shows the example code to achieve this. Add extra compile-only dependencies in the build file of the newly created module.

An example of the implementation is shown in Listing 6-6.

Listing 6-5. The Build File for Portlet Filters

```
dependencies {
        compileOnly group: "com.liferay.portal", name:
        "release.dxp.api"

        cssBuilder group: "com.liferay", name: "com.liferay.
        css.builder", version: "3.0.2"

        compileOnly group: "javax.portlet", name: "portlet-
        api", version: "2.0"
    compileOnly group: "javax.servlet", name: "javax.servlet-
    api", version: "3.0.1"
    compileOnly group: "com.liferay.portal", name:
    "com.liferay.portal.kernel", version: "2.0.0"
    compileOnly group: "org.osgi", name: "osgi.cmpn",
    version: "6.0.0"
}
```

Listing 6-6. The Portlet Filter Implementation Class

```
package com.apress.handsonliferay.portlet;

import com.liferay.portal.kernel.model.PortletFilter;
import com.liferay.portal.kernel.util.PortletKeys;

import java.io.IOException;

import javax.portlet.PortletException;
import javax.portlet.RenderRequest;
import javax.portlet.RenderResponse;
```

```java
import javax.portlet.filter.FilterChain;
import javax.portlet.filter.FilterConfig;
import javax.portlet.filter.RenderFilter;
import javax.portlet.filter.RenderResponseWrapper;

import org.osgi.service.component.annotations.Component;

/**
 * @author Inthiyaz_Apoorva
 */
@Component(
                immediate = true,
                property = {
                        "javax.portlet.name=" +
                        PortletKeys.BLOGS
                },
                service = PortletFilter.class
)
public class MyBlogRenderFilterPortlet implements
RenderFilter {

        @Override
        public void init(FilterConfig filterConfig) throws
        PortletException {
                // TODO Auto-generated method stub

        }

        @Override
        public void destroy() {
                // TODO Auto-generated method stub

        }
```

```java
@Override
public void doFilter(RenderRequest request,
RenderResponse response, FilterChain chain)
            throws IOException, PortletException {
    RenderResponseWrapper renderResponseWrapper =
    new RenderResponseWrapper(response);

    chain.doFilter(request, renderResponseWrapper);

    String text = renderResponseWrapper.toString();

    if (text != null) {
        String interestingText =
        "<input  class=\"field form-control\"";

        int index = text.lastIndexOf
        (interestingText);

        if (index >= 0) {
            String newText1 = text.
            substring(0, index);
            String newText2 = "\n<p>Added by
            MyBlogs Render Filter!</p>\n";
            String newText3 = text.substring
            (index);

            String newText = newText1 + newText2 +
            newText3;

            response.getWriter().write(newText);
        }
    }

    }
}
```

Using OSGi Fragments or a Custom JSP Bag

Liferay strongly recommends customizing JSPs using Liferay DXP's APIs, which you learned about in the previous section. Overriding a JSP using an OSGi fragment or a custom JSP bag comes with limitations, they don't guarantee anything, and there are times when they fail miserably. If there is an issue with the code, the error will appear at runtime. Liferay's official documentation suggests this approach must be used as a last resort.

Using an OSGi Fragment

As it is said, "with great power comes great responsibility." OSGi fragments are an excellent example of this. They are mighty, and they allow you to modify JSPs completely, leading to the customization of the widget's complete look and feel and functionality. They can also make a module fail. If the Liferay DXP patch that modifies a JSP is installed, it can cause this fragment to fail.

An OSGi fragment that overrides a JSP requires these two things:

1. Declare the fragment host. The following code declares the fragment host:

   ```
   "Fragment-Host: com.liferay.login.web;bundle-
   version="[1.0.0,1.0.1)"
   ```

2. Provide the overridden JSP. In the overridden JSP, you have two possible naming conventions for targeting the host's original JSP: portal and original.

   For example, if the original JSP is in the /META-INF/ resources/login.jsp folder, the fragment bundle should contain a JSP with the same path, using this pattern:

   ```
   <liferay-util:include
   page="/login.original.jsp" (or login.portal.jsp)
   servletContext="<%= application %>"
   />
   ```

You must ensure that you mimic the host module's folder structure when overriding its JAR. For example:

```
my-jsp-fragment/src/main/resources/META-INF/
resources/login.jsp
```

If your fragment uses an internal package from the fragment host, continue using it, but you must explicitly exclude the package from the bundle's `Import-Package` OSGi manifest header.

This `Import-Package` header, for example, excludes packages that match `com.liferay.portal.search.web.internal.*`.

Using a Custom JSP Bag

Customization with a custom JSP bag has the same limitation as the OSGi fragment method. Custom JSP bag methods can be used to customize Liferay DXP core JSPs.

This custom JSP Bag module must satisfy the criteria of providing and specifying a custom JSP for the JSP you're extending.

1. Create JSPs to override the Liferay DXP core JSPs. For example, if you're overriding `portal-web/docroot/html/common/themes/bottom-ext.jsp`, you have to place your custom JSP in the following path of your custom module:

    ```
    apressMVC/src/main/resources/META-INF/jsps/
    html/common/themes/bottom-ext.jsp
    ```

Note   If you use a location other than the Liferay core, you have to assign that location to a `-includeresource: META-INF/jsps=` directive in your module's `bnd.bnd` file. For example, if you place custom JSPs in a folder called `src/META-INF/custom_jsps` in your module, you would specify the following in your `bnd.bnd`

file: -includeresource: META-INF/jsps=src/META-INF/
custom_jsps. This includes a CustomJspBag implementation for
serving the custom JSPs.

Listing 6-7 shows example code that will help you achieve the
functionality for CustomJspBags. You can write a class with this code.

Listing 6-7. The CustomJSPBag Implementation Class

```
package com.apress.handsonliferay.portlet;

import com.liferay.portal.deploy.hot.CustomJspBag;
import com.liferay.portal.kernel.url.URLContainer;

import java.net.URL;
import java.util.ArrayList;
import java.util.Enumeration;
import java.util.HashSet;
import java.util.List;
import java.util.Set;

import org.osgi.framework.Bundle;
import org.osgi.framework.BundleContext;
import org.osgi.service.component.annotations.Activate;
import org.osgi.service.component.annotations.Component;

@Component(
        immediate = true,
        property = {
            "context.id=BladeCustomJspBag",
            "context.name=Test Custom JSP Bag",
            "service.ranking:Integer=100"
        }
    )
```

```java
public class MycustomJSPBAG implements CustomJspBag {

        private Bundle _bundle;
        private List<String> _customJsps;

        @Override
        public String getCustomJspDir() {
                return "META-INF/jsps/";
        }

        @Activate
        protected void activate(BundleContext bundleContext) {
                _bundle = bundleContext.getBundle();

                _customJsps = new ArrayList<>();

                Enumeration<URL> entries = _bundle.findEntries(
                        getCustomJspDir(), "*.jsp", true);

                while (entries.hasMoreElements()) {
                        URL url = entries.nextElement();

                        _customJsps.add(url.getPath());
                }
        }
        @Override
        public List<String> getCustomJsps() {
                return _customJsps;
        }

        @Override
        public URLContainer getURLContainer() {
                return _urlContainer;
        }
```

```
private final URLContainer _urlContainer = new
URLContainer() {

    @Override
    public URL getResource(String name) {
        return _bundle.getEntry(name);
    }
    @Override
    public Set<String> getResources(String path) {
        Set<String> paths = new HashSet<>();

        for (String entry : _customJsps) {
            if (entry.startsWith(path)) {
                paths.add(entry);
            }
        }

        return paths;
    }
};

    @Override
    public boolean isCustomJspGlobal() {
            return true;
    }
}
```

This sample code should help you understand the CustomJspBag.

There is one more concept called ExtendJSP, which can also be used to override JSPs.

If you want to add something to a Liferay core JSP, you have to create an empty JSP with a postfix of -ext jsp and then override that instead of the whole JSP, which will help avoid the confusion and not mess up the actual code. This approach keeps things more straightforward and stable and helps prevent breaking your customization.

Using this concept, you only rely on the original JSP, including the -ext.jsp file.

For example, open `portal-web/docroot/html/common/themes/bottom.jsp` and scroll to the end. You'll see this:

```
<liferay-util:include page="/html/common/themes/bottom-
ext.jsp" />
```

If you must add something to `bottom.jsp`, you must override `bottom-ext.jsp`.

This section has explained how to customize JSPs. In the next section, you learn how to customize services using wrappers.

Customizing Services Using Wrappers

There are cases in real-world applications where you need certain extra functionality on top of the out-of-box Liferay features. For example, you saw how to change the word "user" to the word "employee" using the language property key. Now assume you are developing a portal that serves as a solution for employees. In this case, the User entity needs to store an Employee ID, which is not a Liferay DXP-provided field in the User entity. To accommodate this scenario, you need to modify the User model. Liferay DXP's service wrappers provide easy-to-use extension points for customizing OOB services.

To create a module for customizing services using wrappers, you need to create a `servicewrapper` module using the Service Wrapper template.

You learn how to do this with the help of an example, which is shown in Figures 6-3 and 6-4 and Listings 6-8 and 6-9.

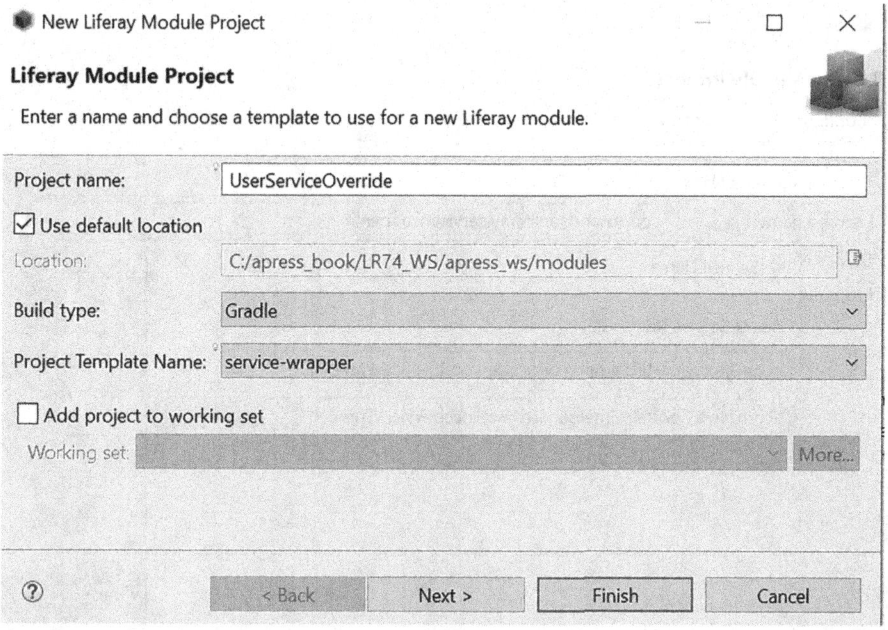

Figure 6-3. Creating the servicewrapper module

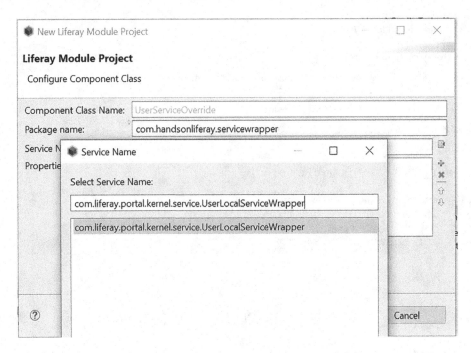

Figure 6-4. *Selecting a user service to override*

Click the Next button in the popup window shown in Figure 6-3.

Listing 6-8. The UserServiceOverride Class

```
package com.handsonliferay.servicewrapper;

import com.liferay.portal.kernel.exception.PortalException;
import com.liferay.portal.kernel.model.User;
import com.liferay.portal.kernel.service.ServiceContext;
import com.liferay.portal.kernel.service.ServiceWrapper;
import com.liferay.portal.kernel.service.UserLocalService;
import com.liferay.portal.kernel.service.
UserLocalServiceWrapper;

import java.util.Locale;
import java.util.Map;
```

```
import org.osgi.service.component.annotations.Component;
import org.osgi.service.component.annotations.Reference;

/**
 * @author Apoorva_Inthiyaz
 */
@Component(
        immediate = true,
        property = {
        },
        service = ServiceWrapper.class
)
public class UserServiceOverride extends
UserLocalServiceWrapper {

        public UserServiceOverride() {
                super(null);
        }
}
```

Listing 6-9. The Customized User Service Wrapper Using the UserServiceOverride Class

```
package com.handsonliferay.servicewrapper;

import com.liferay.portal.kernel.exception.PortalException;
import com.liferay.portal.kernel.model.User;
import com.liferay.portal.kernel.service.ServiceContext;
import com.liferay.portal.kernel.service.ServiceWrapper;
import com.liferay.portal.kernel.service.UserLocalService;
import com.liferay.portal.kernel.service.
UserLocalServiceWrapper;

import java.util.Locale;
import java.util.Map;
```

```java
import org.osgi.service.component.annotations.Component;
import org.osgi.service.component.annotations.Reference;

/**
 * @author Apoorva_Inthiyaz
 */
@Component(
        immediate = true,
        property = {
        },
        service = ServiceWrapper.class
)
public class UserServiceOverride extends
UserLocalServiceWrapper {

        public UserServiceOverride() {
                super(null);
        }

        @Override
                public User addUser(long creatorUserId,
                long companyId, boolean autoPassword,
                String password1, String password2,boolean
                autoScreenName, String screenName, String
                emailAddress, Locale locale, String
                firstName,String middleName, String lastName,
                long prefixId, long suffixId, boolean male,
                int birthdayMonth,int birthdayDay, int
                birthdayYear, String jobTitle, long[] groupIds,
                long[] organizationIds, long[] roleIds,long[]
                userGroupIds, boolean sendEmail, ServiceContext
                serviceContext) throws PortalException {
                        // TODO Auto-generated method stub
```

216

```
System.out.println(" User First Name
"+firstName);
System.out.println(" User middle Name
"+middleName);
System.out.println("User Last Name "+lastName);

            return super.addUser(creatorUserId,
            companyId, autoPassword, password1,
            password2, autoScreenName,
            screenName,emailAddress, locale,
            firstName, middleName, lastName,
            prefixId, suffixId, male, birthdayMonth,
            birthdayDay,birthdayYear, jobTitle,
            groupIds, organizationIds,
            roleIds, userGroupIds, sendEmail,
            serviceContext);
    }

@Override
public User getUser(long userId) throws
PortalException {
    System.out.println("Getting user by id " + userId);
    return super.getUser(userId);
}

@Reference(unbind = "-")
private void serviceSetter(UserLocalService
userLocalService) {
    setWrappedService(userLocalService);
}
}
```

This section has explained how to customize services using wrappers; in the next section, you learn how to customize OSGi services.

Customizing OSGi Services

Let's rewind a bit to the OSGi chapter, where you learned that all the components are registered as services in the OSGi service registry. All the services builder services existing inside portal implementations (`portal-impl`) are standard spring beans implementations, which Liferay makes available as OSGi services.

This customization approach is tricky because it involves identifying the service extension point for service modification. This can be done with the help of the Gogo shell. Once the service is identified, you need to create a new module with a custom service. And finally, you need to configure the OSGi component to use the newly created service. An important point to note here is the service rank; the custom module must have a higher ranking to make the custom module override a service.

Let's look at an example. Here are the steps to customize an OSGI service:

1. Get the service and service reference details.
   Use the `scr:info [componentName]` command in the Gogo shell and then follow these steps:

   a. Copy the service interface name.

   b. Copy the existing service name.

   c. Gather any reference configuration details (if reconfiguration is necessary).

2. Create a custom service. Follow these steps:

   a. Create a module.

   b. Create a custom service class to implement the service interface you want.

   c. Ensure that the declarative services component is the best match for the reference to the service interface.

d. If you want to use the existing service implementation, declare a field that uses a declarative services reference to the existing service. Use the `component.name` key for that. For example:

```
@Reference  (
        target="(component.name=override.my.service.
        reference.service.impl.SomeServiceImpl)"
        )
private SomeService _defaultService;
```

e. Override the interface methods if required.

f. Deploy the module to register the custom service.

3. Configure components to use your custom service. Liferay DXP's Configuration Admin lets you use configuration files to swap service references on the fly.

a. You need to create a system configuration file with the `[component].config` naming convention, replacing `[component]` with the component's name.

b. Add a reference entry to the `[reference].target=[filter]` file.

c. Use `[Liferay_Home]/osgi/configs` to deploy the configuration file.

This section has explained how to customize OSGi services. In the next section, you see how to customize MVC commands.

Customizing MVC Commands

Chapter 3 covered MVC commands and explained how they work. To summarize, MVC commands allow you to break a single controller class into several classes for each kind of portlet action, making the code more manageable. You learned about the controller class, which is essentially a component class, because of the @component annotation. These classes are registered as OSGi components in the component registry. The basic concept is to create a service with custom code and at a higher ranking that overrides the command. While customizing MVCActionCommand and MVCResourceCommand, you add custom logic to the methods, whereas for MVCRenderCommand, you can redirect users to a different JSP by adding more logic.

Let's look at this more closely with an example.

Here are the steps for adding logic to MVC commands:

1. Implement the interface:

    ```
    public class MVC_Action_Override extends
    BaseMVCActionCommand
    ```

2. Publish this as a component:

    ```
    @Component(
                    immediate = true,
                    property = {
                    "javax.portlet.name=" +
                    BlogsPortletKeys.BLOGS_ADMIN,
                    "mvc.command.name=/blogs/edit_entry",
                    "service.ranking:Integer=100"
                    },
            service = MVCActionCommand.class
        )
    ```

3. Refer to the original implementation:

```
@Reference(target= "(component.name=com.
liferay.blogs.web.internal.portlet.action.
EditEntryMVCActionCommand)")
protected MVCActionCommand mvcActionCommand;
```

4. Add the logic and call the original:

```
@Override
protected void doProcessAction(ActionRequest
actionRequest, ActionResponse actionResponse) throws
Exception {
                // Add your custom logic in this method
                mvcActionCommand.processAction
                (actionRequest, actionResponse);
        }
```

You can see complete implementations of the MVC_Action_Override class in Listing 6-10, the MVC_Resource_Override class in Listing 6-11, and the MVC_Render_Override class in Listing 6-12.

Listing 6-10. MVC_Action_Override Complete Class

```
package com.handsonliferay.mvccommandoverride.portlet;

import com.liferay.blogs.constants.BlogsPortletKeys;
import com.liferay.portal.kernel.portlet.bridges.mvc.
BaseMVCActionCommand;
import com.liferay.portal.kernel.portlet.bridges.mvc.
MVCActionCommand;

import javax.portlet.ActionRequest;
import javax.portlet.ActionResponse;
```

```java
import org.osgi.service.component.annotations.Component;
import org.osgi.service.component.annotations.Reference;

/**
 * @author Apoorva_Inthiyaz
 */
@Component(
        immediate = true,
        property = {
                "javax.portlet.name=" +
                BlogsPortletKeys.BLOGS_ADMIN,
                "mvc.command.name=/blogs/edit_entry",
                "service.ranking:Integer=100"
                },
        service = MVCActionCommand.class
)
public class MVC_Action_Override extends BaseMVCActionCommand {

        @Override
        protected void doProcessAction(ActionRequest
        actionRequest, ActionResponse actionResponse) throws
        Exception {
                // Add your custom logic in this method
                mvcActionCommand.processAction(actionRequest,
                actionResponse);
        }
        @Reference(
                target = "(component.name=com.liferay.
                blogs.web.internal.portlet.action.
                EditEntryMVCActionCommand)")
                protected MVCActionCommand mvcActionCommand;
}
```

Listing 6-11. MVC_Resource_Override Complete Class

```
package com.handsonliferay.mvccommandoverride.portlet;

import com.liferay.login.web.constants.LoginPortletKeys;
import com.liferay.portal.kernel.portlet.bridges.mvc.
MVCResourceCommand;

import javax.portlet.PortletException;
import javax.portlet.ResourceRequest;
import javax.portlet.ResourceResponse;

import org.osgi.service.component.annotations.Component;
import org.osgi.service.component.annotations.Reference;

/**
 * @author Apoorva_Inthiyaz
 */
@Component(
            property = {
                "javax.portlet.name=" + LoginPortletKeys.LOGIN,
                "mvc.command.name=/login/captcha"
            },
            service = MVCResourceCommand.class
)
public class MVC_Resource_Override implements MVCResourceCommand{

    @Reference(target =
            "(component.name=com.liferay.login.web.internal.
            portlet.action.CaptchaMVCResourceCommand)")
        protected MVCResourceCommand mvcResourceCommand;

        @Override
        public boolean serveResource(ResourceRequest
        resourceRequest, ResourceResponse resourceResponse)
                        throws PortletException {
```

```
                    System.out.println("Serving login captcha
                    image");

                    return mvcResourceCommand.serveResource
                    (resourceRequest, resourceResponse);
        }
}
```

Listing 6-12. MVC_Render_Override Complete Class

```
package com.handsonliferay.mvccommandoverride.portlet;

import com.liferay.blogs.constants.BlogsPortletKeys;
import com.liferay.portal.kernel.portlet.bridges.mvc.
MVCRenderCommand;
import com.liferay.portal.kernel.portlet.bridges.mvc.constants.
MVCRenderConstants;
import com.liferay.portal.kernel.util.PortalUtil;

import javax.portlet.PortletException;
import javax.portlet.RenderRequest;
import javax.portlet.RenderResponse;
import javax.servlet.RequestDispatcher;
import javax.servlet.ServletContext;
import javax.servlet.http.HttpServletRequest;
import javax.servlet.http.HttpServletResponse;

import org.osgi.service.component.annotations.Component;
import org.osgi.service.component.annotations.Reference;

/**
 * @author Apoorva_Inthiyaz
 */
@Component(
            immediate = true,
```

```
        property = {
            "javax.portlet.name=" + BlogsPortletKeys.BLOGS,
            "javax.portlet.name=" +
            BlogsPortletKeys.BLOGS_ADMIN,
            "javax.portlet.name=" + BlogsPortletKeys.BLOGS_
            AGGREGATOR,
            "mvc.command.name=/blogs/edit_entry"
        },
        service = MVCRenderCommand.class
    )
public class MVC_Render_Override implements MVCRenderCommand {

    @Override
        public String render(
            RenderRequest renderRequest, RenderResponse
            renderResponse) throws
                PortletException {

            System.out.println("Rendering custom_edit_
            entry.jsp");

            RequestDispatcher requestDispatcher =
                servletContext.getRequestDispatcher
                ("/custom_edit_entry.jsp");

            try {
                HttpServletRequest httpServletRequest =
                    PortalUtil.getHttpServletRequest(rende
                    rRequest);
                HttpServletResponse httpServletResponse =
                    PortalUtil.getHttpServletResponse
                    (renderResponse);
```

```
                   requestDispatcher.include
                       (httpServletRequest, httpServletResponse);
               } catch (Exception e) {
                   throw new PortletException
                       ("Unable to include custom_edit_entry.
                       jsp", e);
               }

               return MVCRenderConstants.MVC_PATH_VALUE_SKIP_
               DISPATCH;
       }

       @Reference(target = "(osgi.web.symbolicname=com.
       custom.code.web)")
       protected ServletContext servletContext;

       @Reference(target = "(component.name=com.
       liferay.blogs.web.internal.portlet.action.
       EditEntryMVCRenderCommand)")
       protected MVCRenderCommand mvcRenderCommand;
}
```

This section has explained how to customize MVC commands. In the next section, you learn how to customize models using model listeners.

Customizing Models Using Model Listeners

Model listeners are classes that listen and invoke alongside model persistent methods and execute certain business logic. Model listeners are generally lightweight logic execution. They must implement the ModelListener interface. Depending on the configuration, this logic execution may occur before or after the model persistence method invocation. However, there are more ways to listen than using the Before and After.

- onBeforeAddAssociation(),
  onAfterAddAssociation(), onBeforeCreate(),
  and onAfterCreate(): These methods are
  invoked when a CREATE operation is intercepted
  on a model. onBeforeAddAssociation() and
  onAfterAddAssociation() are used when mapping
  exists between two entities. These methods can be
  used to execute logic before/after an association
  record is added. For one table, onBeforeCreate() and
  onAfterCreate() are invoked after/before the creation
  of a single table record.

- onBeforeUpdate() and onAfterUpdate():These
  methods are invoked when an UPDATE operation is
  intercepted.

- onBeforeRemoveAssociation(),
  onAfterRemoveAssociation(), onBeforeRemove(),
  and onAfterRemove(): These methods are
  invoked when a DELETE operation is intercepted
  on a model. onBeforeRemoveAssociation() and
  onAfterRemoveAssociation() are used when mapping
  tables exist between two entities. These methods can
  be used to execute logic before/after an association
  record is deleted. For one table, onBeforeRemove() and
  onAfterRemove() are invoked before/after the creation
  of a single table record.

You can understand this process with the help of Figure 6-5.

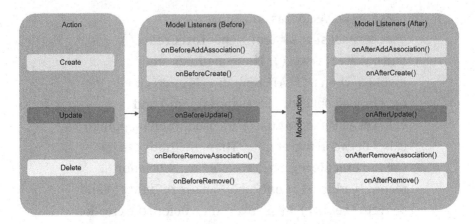

Figure 6-5. *The order of the model listener evets*

In a previous example, you saw how to add the Employee Id field to the User entity. Now let's look at the same example of an employee, but this time you need to print an audit log in the logging file whenever a new user is added to the Liferay database. Listing 6-13 shows a sample implementation.

Listing 6-13. Custom Entity Listener Class

```
package com.handsonliferay.mvccommandoverride.portlet;

import com.handsonliferay.apress_service_builder.model.
ApressBook;
import com.liferay.portal.kernel.model.BaseModel;
import com.liferay.portal.kernel.model.BaseModelListener;
import com.liferay.portal.kernel.model.ModelListener;

import org.osgi.service.component.annotations.Component;

/**
 * @author Apoorva_Inthiyaz
 */
```

```
@Component(
            immediate = true,
            service = ModelListener.class
)
public class CustomEntityListener extends
BaseModelListener<ApressBook>{

}
```

This section has explained how to customize MVC commands and customizing models using model listeners. In the next section, you see how to implement Expando attributes.

Expando Attributes

Expando attributes, as the name suggests, are used to expand something. In Liferay, Expando attributes are often referred to as custom fields. These fields are essentially extra fields that can be added to Liferay's OOB entities. The best part of using this Liferay feature is that these fields can be added without modifying the table but by doing it logically. The data saved in these fields is available on-demand, similar to other preexisting fields' data.

These custom fields can be added to the control panel as well. Expando also provides APIs to manage tables, columns, rows, and values programmatically. Liferay's database contains four tables to save these custom attribute values for persistence—expandotable, expandorow, expandocolumn and expandovalue—as shown in Figures 6-6 through 6-9.

Figure 6-6. *The expandotable table view*

Figure 6-7. *The expandorow table view*

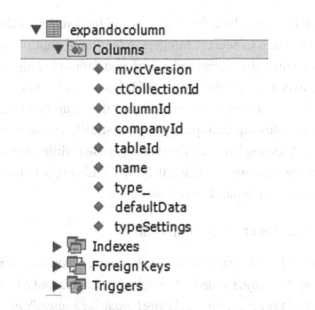

Figure 6-8. *The expandocolumn table view*

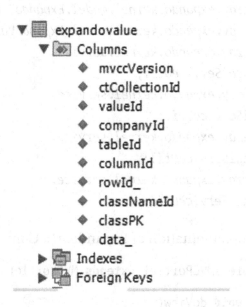

Figure 6-9. *The expandovalue table view*

Custom fields can be different types and hold various values, such as text fields (indexed or secret), integers, selection of multiple values, and many more. Once you've created a field, you cannot change its type.

Expando is a compelling feature of Liferay, and it adds a lot of flexibility for developers to utilize existing entities and add features on top of them. The following example programmatically operates on a custom field. You can see the list of all the packages used while programmatically implementing Expando in Listing 6-14, while Listing 6-15 has a complete implementation of Expando in an action class.

Listing 6-14. Packages for Expando

```
import com.liferay.expando.kernel.model.ExpandoColumn;
import com.liferay.expando.kernel.model.ExpandoColumnConstants;
import com.liferay.expando.kernel.model.ExpandoRow;
import com.liferay.expando.kernel.model.ExpandoTable;
import com.liferay.expando.kernel.model.ExpandoTableConstants;
import com.liferay.expando.kernel.model.ExpandoValue;
import com.liferay.expando.kernel.service.
ExpandoColumnLocalServiceUtil;
import com.liferay.expando.kernel.service.
ExpandoRowLocalServiceUtil;
import com.liferay.expando.kernel.service.
ExpandoTableLocalServiceUtil;
import com.liferay.expando.kernel.service.
ExpandoValueLocalServiceUtil;
```

Listing 6-15. Implementation of Expando in a Controller Class

```
public class ApressMVCPortlet extends MVCPortlet {

        public void doView(
```

```java
        RenderRequest renderRequest, RenderResponse
        renderResponse)
throws IOException, PortletException {

        System.out.println("START... Process Expando...");
        ThemeDisplay themeDisplay = (ThemeDisplay)
        renderRequest.getAttribute(WebKeys.THEME_DISPLAY);

        ExpandoTable userExpandoTable = getOrAddExpando
        Table(themeDisplay.getCompanyId(), User.class.
        getName(),
                    ExpandoTableConstants.DEFAULT_
                    TABLE_NAME);

        System.out.println("User Expando Table ID : " +
        userExpandoTable.getTableId());

        ExpandoColumn designationExpandoColumn = getOr
        AddExpandoColumn(themeDisplay.getCompanyId(),
        User.class.getName(),
                    ExpandoTableConstants.DEFAULT_TABLE_
                    NAME, "Designation", userExpandoTable);

        System.out.println("Designation Expando Column ID :
        " + designationExpandoColumn.getColumnId());
        System.out.println("DONE... Process Expando...");
        include(viewTemplate, renderRequest,
        renderResponse);
    }

    public ExpandoTable getOrAddExpandoTable(long
    companyId, String className, String tableName) {
        ExpandoTable expandoTable = null;
        try {
```

```
        expandoTable = ExpandoTableLocalServiceUtil.
        getDefaultTable(companyId, className);
    } catch (NoSuchTableException e) {
        try {
            expandoTable = ExpandoTableLocalServiceUtil
            .addTable(companyId, className, tableName);
        } catch (Exception e1) {
        }
    } catch (Exception e) {
        System.out.println(e);
    }
    return expandoTable;
}

public ExpandoColumn getOrAddExpandoColumn(long
companyId, String className, String tableName, String
columnName,
        ExpandoTable expandoTable) {
    ExpandoColumn exandoColumn = null;
    try {
        exandoColumn = ExpandoColumnLocalServiceUtil
        .getColumn(companyId, className, tableName,
        columnName);
        if (exandoColumn == null) {
            exandoColumn = ExpandoColumnLocalServiceU
            til.addColumn(expandoTable.getTableId(),
            columnName,
                    ExpandoColumnConstants.STRING,
                    StringPool.BLANK);
        }
    } catch (SystemException e) {
        System.out.println(e);
```

```
        } catch (PortalException e) {
            System.out.println(e);
        }
        return exandoColumn;
    }

    public ExpandoRow getOrAddExpandoRow(long tableId,long
    rowId , long classPK) {
        ExpandoRow expandoRow = null;
        try {
                expandoRow = ExpandoRowLocalService
                Util.getRow(rowId);
                if(expandoRow ==null) {
                expandoRow        = ExpandoRowLocal
                ServiceUtil.addRow(tableId, classPK);
                }
        } catch (PortalException e) {
                // TODO Auto-generated catch block
                e.printStackTrace();
        }
        return expandoRow;
    }
    public void getExpandoValue(long companyId,long
    classNameId, long tableName) {

            ExpandoValue expandoValue =  ExpandoValueLoca
            lServiceUtil.getValue(companyId, classNameId,
            tableName);
    }

}
```

This section has explained how to implement Expando attributes. In the next section, you see how to implement post- and pre-actions.

Pre and Post-Actions

Pre- and post-actions are essential features and come in handy when you need to execute certain logic before (*pre*) or after (*post*) the execution of the auction event. This process of writing pre- and post-actions is also called *event customization*. The following is the list of portal events that can be customized using this approach:

- application. startup.events, application. shutdown.events

- login.events.pre, login.events.post

- logout.events.pre, logout.events.post

- servlet.service.events.pre, servlet.service. events.post

- servlet.session.create.events, servlet.session. destroy.events

Portal.properties contain information about portal events, which is why you need to extend the portal.properties file to implement this. Hooks are instrumental in implementing these scenarios. They are good for triggering custom actions on common portal events, such as user logins or system startups. The actions for each of these events are defined in portal.properties, so you need to extend this file to create a custom action. Hooks make this a simple task.

Let's look at this more deeply with an example. Figure 6-10 shows how to create a component class.

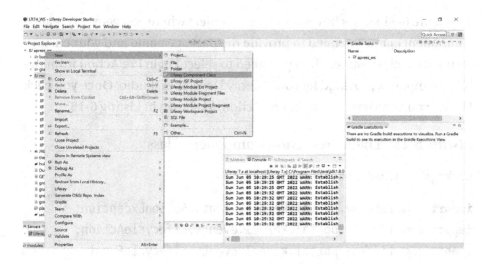

Figure 6-10. *Menu to create a Liferay component class*

Right-click the module and then choose New ➤ Liferay Component Class, as shown in Figure 6-10.

New Liferay Component

New Liferay Component

Create a new Liferay Component Class

Project name:	MVC_Command_Override
Package name:	com.handsonliferay.preaction
Component Class Name:	MyPreAction
Component Class Template:	Login Pre Action

< Back   Next >   Finish   Cancel

Figure 6-11. *Selecting the component class template for a pre-action*

Figure 6-11 shows how to select any project where you want to create a component class. You need to provide the package name and your custom component class name. Then you need to select Login Pre Action from the list of templates provided by your Liferay Developer Studio. Once you click Finish, you can view the Login Pre-Action, as shown in Listing 6-16.

Listing 6-16. Login Pre-Action Component Class

```
package com.handsonliferay.preaction;

import com.liferay.portal.kernel.events.ActionException;
import com.liferay.portal.kernel.events.LifecycleAction;
import com.liferay.portal.kernel.events.LifecycleEvent;
import org.osgi.service.component.annotations.Component;

@Component(
        immediate = true,
        property = {
                "key=login.events.pre"
        },
        service = LifecycleAction.class
)
public class MyPreAction implements LifecycleAction {

        @Override
        public void processLifecycleEvent(LifecycleEvent
        lifecycleEvent)
                throws ActionException {

                System.out.println("login.event.pre=" +
                lifecycleEvent);

        }

}
```

The processLifecycleEvent method will be executed before the login action is performed:

```
@Component(
        immediate = true,
        property = {
                "key=login.events.pre"
        },
        service = LifecycleAction.class
)
```

The component section from the class shows which type of action class you are using, pre or post. If you want to create an action for post, your key value will change, as shown in Listing 6-17.

Listing 6-17. Login Post-Action Component Class

```
package com.handsonliferay.postaction;

import com.liferay.portal.kernel.events.ActionException;
import com.liferay.portal.kernel.events.LifecycleAction;
import com.liferay.portal.kernel.events.LifecycleEvent;
import org.osgi.service.component.annotations.Component;

@Component(
        immediate = true,
        property = {
                "key=login.events.post"
        },
        service = LifecycleAction.class
)
public class MyPostAction implements LifecycleAction {

        @Override
```

```
public void processLifecycleEvent(LifecycleEvent
lifecycleEvent)
        throws ActionException {

        System.out.println("login.event.post=" +
        lifecycleEvent);
    }

}
```

This section has explained how to implement post- and pre-actions. In the next section, you see how to customize search.

Customizing Search

Search is a new term in the book and has not been covered in any previous sections. Search basically involves a search engine that uses algorithms and indexes to fetch relevant results based on entered search terms. A scoring method is used to decide the relevancy of the results, which is referred to as *ranking*. The higher the rank, the more relevant the result is. It helps to have a high-speed mechanism to calculate rank every time the user enters a new search term, which is why this cannot be performed in the database. Search engines use *indexes* for this purpose which are fast for these kinds of tasks. These indexes store data per the search execution and querying logic.

Elasticsearch and Solr search are supported search engines in Liferay DXP, Elasticsearch being the default one. These search engines can be deployed on differents server or on the same server. The first approach is called *remote mode*, while the second is called *embedded*. Liferay recommends using remote search mode for production.

To enable search in your custom modules, Liferay provides a search API. To make your custom model (hereafter referred to as the *custom asset*) searchable, you need to save it in the Liferay search index. To achieve this, you must make sure it implements a model document contributor.

There is much more to understand about search, and it could fill a whole book. So, without deviating too much from the point, let's look at a simple example of how you can enable search in a custom module.

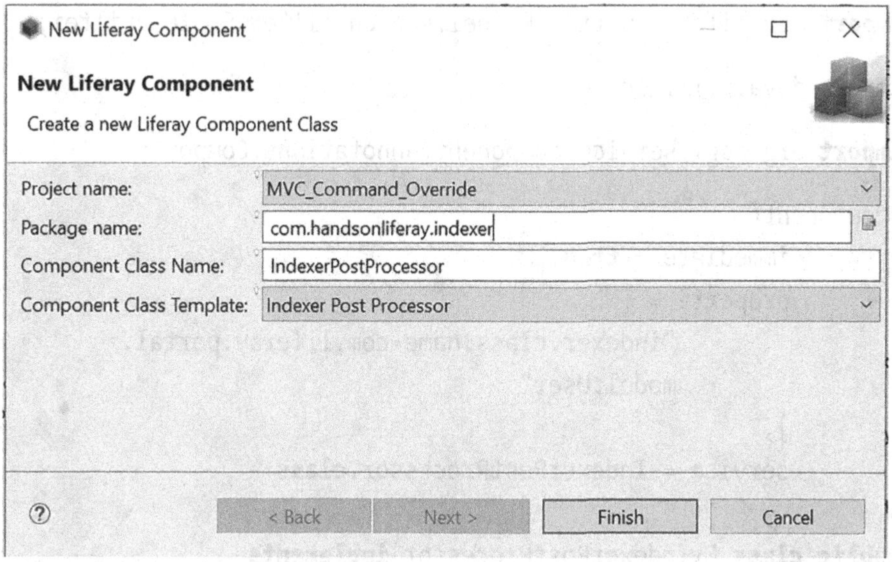

Figure 6-12. *Selecting the component class template for indexer*

Figure 6-12 shows how to select any project where you want to create a component class. You need to provide the package name and your custom component class name. Then you need to select Indexer Post Processor from the list of templates provided by your Liferay Developer Studio. Once you click Finish, you can view MyIndexerPostProcessor, as shown in Listing 6-18.

Listing 6-18. MyIndexerPostProcessor Component Default Class

```
package com.handsonliferay.indexer;

import com.liferay.portal.kernel.log.Log;
import com.liferay.portal.kernel.log.LogFactoryUtil;
import com.liferay.portal.kernel.search.BooleanQuery;
```

```java
import com.liferay.portal.kernel.search.Document;
import com.liferay.portal.kernel.search.IndexerPostProcessor;
import com.liferay.portal.kernel.search.SearchContext;
import com.liferay.portal.kernel.search.Summary;
import com.liferay.portal.kernel.search.filter.BooleanFilter;

import java.util.Locale;

import org.osgi.service.component.annotations.Component;

@Component(
        immediate = true,
        property = {
                "indexer.class.name=com.liferay.portal.
                model.User"
        },
        service = IndexerPostProcessor.class
)
public class MyIndexerPostProcessor implements
IndexerPostProcessor {

        @Override
        public void postProcessContextBooleanFilter(
                        BooleanFilter booleanFilter,
                        SearchContext searchContext)
                throws Exception {
                if (_log.isInfoEnabled()) {
                        _log.info("postProcessContextBoolean
                        Filter");
                }
        }
        @Override
```

```java
public void postProcessDocument(Document document,
Object obj)
        throws Exception {
        if (_log.isInfoEnabled()) {
                _log.info("postProcessDocument");
        }
}

@Override
public void postProcessFullQuery(
                BooleanQuery fullQuery, SearchContext
                searchContext)
        throws Exception {

        if (_log.isInfoEnabled()) {
                _log.info("postProcessFullQuery");
        }
}

@Override
public void postProcessSearchQuery(
                BooleanQuery searchQuery, BooleanFilter
                booleanFilter, SearchContext
                searchContext)
        throws Exception {

        if (_log.isInfoEnabled()) {
                _log.info("postProcessSearchQuery");
        }
}

@Override
public void postProcessSummary(
```

```
                     Summary summary, Document document, Locale
                     locale, String snippet) {

                if (_log.isInfoEnabled()) {
                        _log.info("postProcessSummary");
                }

        }

        private static final Log _log = LogFactoryUtil.getLog(
            MyIndexerPostProcessor.class);

}
```

Listing 6-18 shows MyIndexerPostProcessor implementing the
IndexerPostProcessor interface, which is provided to customize search
queries and documents before they're sent to the search engine, and
to customize result summaries when they're returned to end users.
This basic demonstration prints a message in the log when one of the
*IndexerPostProcessor methods is called.

You must add a logging category to the portal to see this sample's
messages in Liferay DXP's log. Navigate to Control Panel ➤ Configuration
➤ Server Administration and choose Log Levels ➤ Add Category. Then fill
out the form as follows:

1. Logger name: com.handsonliferay.indexer.
    MyIndexerPostProcessor

2. Log level: INFO

```
    @Component(
            immediate = true,
            property = {
```

```
        "indexer.class.name=com.liferay.portal.
        model.User"
    },
    service = IndexerPostProcessor.class
)
```

The component section from the component class is written for the User model. If you want to write an indexer for a custom model, you have to use the indexer class name of the custom model.

For example:

```
property = {
"indexer.class.name=com.handsonliferay.apress_
service_builder.model.ApressBook
        },
```

Summary

This is the last chapter of this book, and you have seen how to customize Liferay differently. You have seen how to customize UI with different methods. Further, you learned about the customization of action classes and services using wrappers, MVC action commands, and models. Finally, you learned how to customize Liferay events and add your module in Search. These all come in very handy in real-world applications.

Index

A

Action command, 89–91
Advanced liferay concepts
    inter-portlet
        communication, 107
    message bus, 107
Apache Felix Gogo Shell, 42
ApressMVC portlet, 61, 62, 64, 67,
        68, 72, 73, 77, 78, 81, 83, 86,
        90, 95, 96, 97
ApressMVCRenderCommand
    class, 84, 86

B

Bean portlet, 99
Blade CLI, 24, 32, 33, 43, 104
Bundle-SymbolicName, 5, 6

C

com.handsonliferay.
    employee.api, 8
Compilation, 30
@Component annotation, 13, 29,
    31, 197, 220
Contexts and Dependency
    Injection (CDI), 99

Controller class, 45, 51, 71,
    185, 220
createActionURL method, 55
createRenderURL method, 55
CRUD (Create, Read, Update and
    Delete) operations, 48,
    173–175, 194
Custom asset, 240
Customizing JSPs
    JSP bag, 208, 209, 211
    Liferay API
        dynamic includes, 201–203
        porlet filters, 204
    OSGi fragment, 207, 208

D

Database connectivity
    via JNDI, 40
    with Liferay DXP, 37–42
    from portal-ext.properties, 39
    RDBMS to Liferay DXP, 38
    from the UI, 38, 39
    web application, 37
Declarative services (DS),
    12, 16, 18
Deployment, 2, 4, 12, 30, 32,
    34, 64, 99

Developer Studio, 24, 31, 61, 63, 65, 154, 155, 157

DS service components, 13

DynamicInclude interface, 203

DynamicQuery API, 179

E

Elasticsearch, 240

Event customization, 236

Expando attributes, 229–232, 235

F

Felix Gogo shell, 43

Finder methods, 160, 176, 178, 181, 182

G

Generated wrapper environment, 23

GenericPortlet class, 52, 53, 58

Global language properties, 195–197

Gogo shell, 100–103

    Balde CLI, 104

    command-line interface for OSGi, 42

    control panel, 103, 104

    Felix Gogo shell, 43

    implementation, 42

    installed bundles list, 44

    in Liferay DXP, 43

    and UNIX Bash shell, 43

Gradle, 23–26, 32, 60, 61, 63, 154, 173

Groovy-based Domain Specific Language (DSL), 26

H

Hibernate, 152

Hypersonic SQL (HSQL), 37

I

IndexerPostProcessor interface, 241, 244

Internationalization, 195

Inter-portlet communication (IPC), 46, 47

    client-side, Ajax, 131, 132

    client-side, cookies, 132, 133

    Private Session Attributes (PSA), 117, 119, 120, 122

    process, 108

    Public Render Parameters (PRPs), 108, 109, 111, 112, 115, 116

    server-side events, 123, 124, 126, 127, 129–131

J, K

Java applications, 2, 5, 40

Java Naming and Directory Interface (JNDI), 38, 40

Java software framework, 1
JSF portlet, 99

L

lb apress command, 102, 104
Liferay component class, 237
Liferay Developer Studiom, 24, 43,
     59, 63, 153, 238, 241
Liferay DXP, 23
    modules, 26
    Tomcat bundle, 33, 34
Liferay DXP-supported build
     tools, 26, 31
Liferay module, 29, 30
    @Component annotation, 31
Liferay Project SDK installer, 32
Liferay's message bus
    asynchronous message bus,
         142, 144, 145
    components, 133
    DestinationListenerRegistrator
         Class, 138–140
    Message Bus API, 133
    MessageBusRegistrator
         Class, 135–137
    schedulers, 145–148
    synchronous message bus,
         140, 142
Liferay's OSGi
    architecture, 19, 20
Liferay Soy portlet, 99
Liferay Theme Generator, 24
Liferay workspace, 24, 25

build tools, 26
    Gradle, 26
    Maven, 27
directory structure, 24, 25
scripts and configurations, 24
Localization, 195

M

Maven, 23, 24, 26–29, 32
Maximized Window State, 52
Minimized Window State, 52
Model listeners, 226–229
Model View Controller (MVC), 58
    commands
        action, 87–91
        render, 82, 84, 86, 87
        resource, 91, 93, 95
    create Liferay, 59–63
    layers, 58
    modules, 59
    understand Liferay, 64, 65, 67
    URL, 67
        action, 73, 75, 77
        render, 67–73
        resource, 78, 80–82
    Window state, 96–98
Module language properties, 195,
     198, 199
MVC commands, 220, 221, 223–226

N

Normal Window State, 52

O

Object-relational mapping (ORM), 152, 153, 194

Open Services Gateway Initiative (OSGi), 1
  benefits, OSGi framework, 21, 22
  bundle, 3
  components, 12–14
  container, 2
  features, 20
  handling dependencies, 3
  Liferay's, 19, 20
  service-oriented development model, 2
  Service Registry, 3
  tools, 21

OSGi Alliance, 1

OSGi architecture, 3
  bundle, 4
  execution environment, 5
  lifecycle layer, 4
  modules, 5
  security, 5
  service gateway, 4
  services layer, 4

OSGi bundles, 4
  bundle rules, 7, 8
  bundle's lifecycle, 5, 9, 12
  bundle states, 10–12
  Bundle-SymbolicName, 6
  Bundle-Version: 1.2.3.2022, 6
  importing bundles, 8
  manifest headers, 5

OSGi @Component Declaration, 14
OSGi Service Platform, 1
OSGi service registry, 218, 219
OSGi services
  declarative services, 16
  Java class/interface, 14
  service Implementation, 15
  service interface, 14, 15
  Service Registry, 16, 17
  standard declarative service annotations, 18

P, Q

Plain old Java objects (POJOs), 100
portal.properties file, 236
Portlet lifecycle, 48
Portlets, 45
  annotations, 52
  Java standard, 52
  lifecycle, 47, 49
  modes, 51
  MVC, 58 (*see also* Model View Controller (MVC))
  page layout view, 46
  request and response, 56, 57
  specifications, 47
  types, 50
  URL, 55
  window state, 51, 52
Post-Action Component Class, 239
Pre-Action Component Class, 238
Pre- and post-actions, 236, 237, 239

Private Session Attributes (PSA),
117, 119, 120, 122
Public Render Parameters (PRPs),
108, 109, 111, 112, 115, 116

R

Ranking, 240
@Referance annotation, 13
Remote mode, 240
Render command, 84, 86, 87
Resource command, 93, 95

S

Search, 240–245
Service Builder
apress_service_builder, 162
build service, 161
creation, 153
CRUD (Create, Read, Update
and Delete)
operations, 173–175
customization via
implementation
classes, 165–171
custom SQL, 181–184
database, 151, 163
Developer Studio, 157
dynamic query, 179
finder methods, 176, 178
generate service classes, 160

Gradle's Build Service task, 160
GUI section, 157
GUI tool, 158, 159
headless REST APIs, 185–191
Liferay Service Layer, 164
plain web/REST
services, 191–194
relational model mapping, 152
remote service implementation,
171, 172
remote services, 185
service classes, 161
service.xml file, 151, 153,
155, 156
SQL statement, 163
Service Component Runtime (SCR)
registers, 16
service handling, 13
service registration, 13
servicewrapper module, 212,
213, 217
Solr search, 240
Spring MVC portlet, 98

T

Tomcat bundled, 33

U, V, W, X, Y, Z

UserServiceOverride Class,
214, 215

Printed in the United States
by Baker & Taylor Publisher Services